Winning Casino Gambling

To Mary & Robin,

I LITRALLY just got this from my publicist. This is the first one of these I'm signing. But now I've used up all the space with a whole bunch of meaningless claptrap. I wish I'd thought ahead about what I was going to write. That really would've been (continued in next book)

Winning Casino Gambling

Scott Tharler

Thunder Bay
P · R · E · S · S

San Diego, California

Thunder Bay Press

An imprint of the Advantage Publishers Group

THUNDER BAY   5880 Oberlin Drive, San Diego, CA 92121-4794

P · R · E · S · S   www.thunderbaybooks.com

Produced by PRC Publishing

The Chrysalis Building

Bramley Road, London W10 6SP, United Kingdom

An imprint of **Chrysalis** Books Group plc

© 2004 PRC Publishing

All notations of errors or omissions should be addressed to Thunder Bay Press,
Editorial Department, at the above address. All other correspondence (author
inquiries, permissions) concerning the content of this book should be addressed
to PRC Publishing, The Chrysalis Building, Bramley Road, London W10 6SP,
United Kingdom. A member of the Chrysalis Group plc.

Library of Congress Cataloging-in-Publication Data

Tharler, Scott.
  Winning casino gambling / Scott Tharler.
    p. cm.
  ISBN 1-59223-200-0
    1. Gambling. 2. Casinos. I. Title.

  GV1301.T455 2004
  795--dc22   2004055377

Printed and bound in Malaysia

1 2 3 4 5 08 07 06 05 04

Contents

CONTENTS

> "The only good luck many great men ever had was being born with the ability and determination to overcome bad luck."
>
> —*Channing Pollock (1880–1946), U.S. humorist*

Luck (either good or bad) doesn't exist in any real, measurable sense. It's just an attempt at explaining why seemingly chance events happened the way they did or a feeling describing a possible fluctuation in future circumstances. But luck can't actually affect people or cause things to happen. And yet gamblers—by definition, people who take risks—tend to believe in and rely heavily on luck, hoping, wishing, and praying for a particular outcome. Rather than falling victim to this fictitious, mysterious, temporary creature called Luck, a better course of action is to arm oneself, where possible, with skill and knowledge.

Any casino games that could possibly have a positive expectation for players—and there are a few—depend on skill. And the games that leave players at an insurmountable disadvantage can at least have that disadvantage minimized with knowledge. For instance, imagine having the choice to pump gasoline from either of the two fuel pumps seen here. Assuming comparable quality, most people would choose the much cheaper one. Casinos don't mark their bets like this. But with a little knowledge, players can know which wagers are a good deal—and which should be avoided.

Every game in the casino represents a slightly different angle on gambling. It's not just a matter of what the "best" bets are. The game has to fit your personality, risk tolerance, and pocketbook as well. You might not like the crowded, fast-paced action of craps, despite the good odds it offers. Or you might feel out of place at a baccarat table, even though it's easy to play and has a low house edge. Hey, maybe poker isn't your thing. And you really just like the idea of hitting a single number at roulette, even though you know the math is against you. However you feel about the games themselves, you have to agree that gambling in the casino is about decisions. And winning—or at least hopefully breaking even—is all about making the right ones.

The most popular table game is blackjack, which offers a house advantage of less than 1%, and this guide looks at basic strategies, as well as house variations. Another popular place in the casino is by the roulette wheel—this is essentially a guessing game and remains one of the most-played casino games despite its unfavorable odds.

For dice games that rely on luck, defensive play is best. Craps is an exciting game with plenty of wagers to avoid and sic bo is an ancient Chinese pastime, full of tricky bets to master. There are also many card games, from the very simple baccarat to the more complex Let It Ride, which is a spin on the classic five-card stud. The odds vary hugely on all of these games, so each card game featured shows the level of success you can hope for.

Poker is a psychology, skill, and religion unto itself. Each game is a deeply personal battle where strategy and skill help the best player to come out on top. There are many types of poker variations featured here, including Three-Card Poker, video poker, and pai gow poker. For each game, player etiquette is analyzed and there are charts to show what to do in a variety of situations, with advice on bluffing and what to do with a certain hand of cards or particular combination.

Machines can be a great way to get an instant payout, but you have to know which machines to play and how to play a near-perfect strategy, and be able to do it at a fast enough rate to feasibly hit a jackpot within a reasonable amount of time.

One of the best moves you can make is to practice before you get to the casino. That means not only reading books and studying optimal strategies, but also logging hours of actual play. If you're serious about gambling and want to win, invest in some software from a company like ConJelCo (Casino Master) or Wilson (Turbo 7-Card Stud and other great poker titles). You'll not only get practice without having to wager actual money, but solid contextual advice as well.

Don't go into a casino with the notion that you're

there to beat the odds. Sure, you'd like to win more than you lose. But you'll have to do it with whatever odds you play under. Part of that has to do with what bets you choose to make.

And that certainly has to do with what games you choose to play. So what you should be asking yourself is what games you're drawn to. Do you like cards more than dice? Would you rather stick to one game or sample a bunch? Are you intimidated by certain games because they seem too complicated? Just because a particular bet or game is popular doesn't mean it's right for you. You need to pay attention to your own goals as a player.

Perhaps you'd like to maximize your time at the tables. Or simply have fun. Risking money on games of chance is certainly fun, but different players have different tolerances. Where one might want the fast action of craps, another might enjoy the slow drama of pai gow poker. Where one might like to play against the dealer in blackjack, another might like to pit wits against other players in poker. Each game has not only its own rules and strategy, but its own culture. Hopefully by reading this book you'll get a better feel for what kind of gambler you are—and aren't.

Aside from playing smart and knowing your limits, don't forget to have a good time. As Danny Jones (inventor of Caribbean Stud Poker) put it: "Ask any casino what business they're in and they won't tell you they're in the gambling business. They'll say they're in the entertainment business." In other words, walk around. Enjoy the atmosphere. People-watch. See a show. Plan time away from the tables. Make the whole experience fun!

In the end, it's all about knowing your limits. Casinos are a business. They are specifically designed, elaborate environments with the sole purpose of relieving you of your money. Ultimately, winning or losing isn't a matter of choice, but playing smart and having a winning attitude is. So think positive. And good luck!

"If a man who cannot count finds a four-leaf clover, is he lucky?"

—*Stanislaw J. Lec (1909–1966), Polish poet*

DO THE MATH

You certainly don't have to be the world's greatest mathematician to win money gambling, assuming you at least know how to make a bet. But if you intend to make more than a single bet and minimize your losses over time in the casino, it's a good idea to learn a little something about how the numbers work.

Odds

First off, you'll hear the word "odds" bandied about quite a bit. In the purest and simplest sense, the odds refer to the number of positive outcomes divided by the total number of possible outcomes. For instance, since the average die* has only one four on its six sides, the odds of rolling a four (or any single number) in one roll are one divided by six ($\frac{1}{6}$). You might hear those odds expressed interchangeably as "1 in 6," "It has a 0.167 chance," or "It happens 16.67% of the time."

*This is assuming we're dealing with a fair die, not a physically flawed die or a "loaded" die that has been purposefully altered to skew the chance of it landing on certain numbers.

By definition, the odds have to be a positive number between zero (it never happens) and one (it always happens). The upshot being that the sum total of every possible outcome must always equal one (i.e., 1.0 or 100%). It's either heads (50%) or tails (50%). A die rolled will show one or two (0.333); three, four, or five (0.5); or six (0.167). Every card is a spade ($^{13}/_{52}$), heart ($^{13}/_{52}$), diamond ($^{13}/_{52}$), or club ($^{13}/_{52}$). This is important, as it's easier sometimes to figure out the chances of a thing not happening and subtract that result from one.

Another way to convey the odds you've probably heard involves the word "to." As in "5 to 1." That means that five of the six outcomes on a die aren't a four and one is. So if you hear the likelihood is "10 to 1," that means the odds are only one out of eleven or it has a .0909 chance. It'll happen about 9% of the time. Expressed as variables, if something has an "x to y" shot, that means the chances are y (the positive outcomes) out of x + y (total number of outcomes).

It gets confusing sometimes when casinos use the word "for" instead of "to," usually when referring to paying out a bet. Despite sounding similar, they mean completely different things. To better illustrate the point, let's use the example of tossing a coin. I tell you I'll give you 25 cents for every time you flip a quarter and it comes up heads, if you give me a quarter every time it doesn't. Sounds fair enough. The "1 to 1" version would be that you flip your own quarter; if it's heads, I give you one of mine; otherwise, you give me that one. The "2 for 1" version would be that you give me a quarter, then flip a second quarter; if it's heads, I give you two quarters; otherwise, I just keep the first quarter. Are you winning more the second way? No! I'm only giving you two because you already gave me one. But saying that I'll pay "2 for 1" sounds like a higher payout. That's exactly why casinos phrase it like that sometimes, so be careful!

Usually when dealing with a ratio—however it's expressed—it's best to simplify. For instance, a 3 in 9 chance is expressed not as ⅜ but as ⅓. Likewise, the chance is expressed not as "6 to 3" but as "2 to 1." The only reason you'd keep it "6 to 3" would be if it were being compared to another bet, such as 5 to 3.

Probability
Independent and Dependent

Since you already know how to talk about odds, let's take a step back and show you how to best figure them out for yourself. For starters, it's important to know how to distinguish between dependent and independent events.

A single toss of a coin, spin of the roulette wheel, or roll of the dice in craps are examples of independent events. It's often said that the coin, wheel, and dice have no memory. This means that from toss to toss, spin to spin, and roll to roll, each event has nothing to do with the past and doesn't affect the future. Thus, no matter how many times you roll a fair die, the chances of a particular number coming up on the next roll will always be $\frac{1}{6}$.

The rule for figuring multiple independent events—usually indicated by an "or" statement—is to use addition. For example, the chance of rolling a die and seeing a four or a two would be the chance of rolling a four ($\frac{1}{6}$) plus the chance of rolling a two ($\frac{1}{6}$), for a sum of $\frac{2}{6}$, which simplifies to $\frac{1}{3}$. Likewise, the chance of a roll coming up odd (a one, three, or five) would be $\frac{3}{6}$, which simplifies to $\frac{1}{2}$. Naturally, the resulting chance of multiple independent events occurring is greater than each individual event, as there are more possibilities.

By contrast, blackjack and poker are filled with examples of dependent events. Think about the chance of picking a king from an ordinary deck of fifty-two cards. Pretty straightforward, the chances are four out of fifty-two. Without replacing the first card selected, what are your chances of picking a king from the rest of the deck? Depending on whether or not the first card was a king, the chances would be either three or four (the number of kings still left) out of fifty-one (the number of cards left in the deck). The ratio would change with each card pulled. In games like this, with a lot of dependent events, it can be tricky to figure an exact probability—an educated guess may have to do.

The rule for figuring multiple dependent events—
usually indicated by an "and" statement—is to use
multiplication. Based on our information from above,
the chance of pulling a pair of kings from a deck on the
first two cards would be $\frac{4}{52}$ times $\frac{3}{51}$—or, simplifying,
$\frac{1}{13}$ times $\frac{1}{17}$—for a result of $\frac{1}{221}$. The resulting chance of
multiple dependent events occurring is lesser than each
individual event. Mathematically, because multiplying
the denominators (bottom parts of the fractions)
creates a smaller number. And conceptually, because
two separate conditions have to be satisfied.

Getting more advanced, let's combine independent
and dependent events. For instance, what are the
chances of pulling either a jack or a spade on the first
card from the deck? Sounds like an independent events
statement. Since the chance of pulling a jack is 4 in 52
and the chance of pulling a spade is 13 in 52, it seems
like the answer should be 17 in 52. Not quite! After all,
we counted the jack of spades twice, both as a jack
and as a spade. So we need to subtract the case where
both conditions are satisfied. We know it's only one
card in question, which means the correct answer is $\frac{16}{52}$,
simplified to $\frac{4}{13}$. But this was a fairly simple example.
We need a rule that encompasses more complicated
circumstances. And here it is:

To figure the likelihood of multiple independent events, add the likelihoods of each one happening and subtract the likelihood of them all happening. Let's test it on our jack of spades example. The likelihoods of each one happening are $\frac{4}{52}$ and $\frac{13}{52}$, resulting in a sum of $\frac{17}{52}$. Before we multiply them, let's simplify the ratios to $\frac{1}{13}$ and $\frac{1}{4}$, respectively. The numerators multiply (1 x 1) to 1 and the denominators multiply (13 x 4) to 52, for a final product of $\frac{1}{52}$—this is the likelihood of them both happening. Subtracting the product ($\frac{1}{52}$) from the sum ($\frac{17}{52}$), we get $\frac{16}{52}$—it works! (The formula inevitably gets even more complicated when dealing with three or more events, but the principle remains the same.)

Combinations and Permutations

To be honest, combinations and permutations don't factor much into certain popular games (e.g., roulette, baccarat, craps). That's because there are no decisions for you to make during play. You put your bets down and the wheel is spun, cards are dealt, and dice are rolled. Either something favorable or unfavorable happens and there's nothing you can do to change it. But in poker games, for example, combinations come into play all the time.

Let's figure out the chances of getting exactly
one pair in the first three cards dealt from the deck
(very important in a game like three-card poker). Since
any card drawn can pair up, the first card dealt doesn't

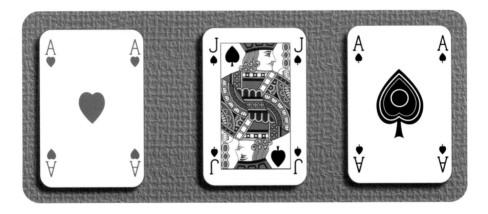

matter. Thus, all fifty-two cards qualify. Only three out
of the fifty-one left match the first one. And forty-eight
of the remaining fifty don't match either of the first
two. (We purposefully want to exclude the chance of a
three of a kind.) Multiplying $^{52}\!/_{52}$ by $^{3}\!/_{51}$ by $^{48}\!/_{50}$, we get a
0.056 chance of making a pair. The reason that seems
really low is because we almost forgot to account for

The House Advantage

The whole point in learning about odds and probability is to gain a better understanding of how they can ultimately impact your wallet. The casino has purposefully designed every game to be profitable for them. What may not be obvious is which bets in which games are better or worse for you, the player. The "house advantage" is a benchmark of how much better or worse a particular bet is likely to be for you over time.

the different combinations. We only based the calculation on the first and second cards matching. But a pair could also happen with the first and third or second and third cards matching. Multiplying by three (the number of combinations), we get 0.169. In other words, a player is likely to be dealt a pair in the first three cards almost 17% of the time. Or to put it another way, if six players are sitting around a table, only one of them is likely to be dealt a pair. (Of

The Vig

Another way the casino ensures it makes a profit is by charging a commission in certain situations. In poker, it might be a percentage of every pot or an hourly fee per player for the privilege of playing there. Games like baccarat and pai gow charge a 5% commission on winning hands. That doesn't mean the house advantage is 5%, because other rules might mitigate that figure. Commissions like these are known as a "vigorish," or "vig" for short.

course, other players could be dealt higher hands, but the combined chances of that happening aren't as great as getting a pair. So any pair is a strong hand in three-card poker.) As you can see, it's always important to consider how different combinations factor in.

To understand the difference between combinations and permutations, let's look at how many ways you could have a pair of sevens when you are dealt three cards. From the last example, we know that there are three possible combinations (7 7 X, 7 X 7, X 7 7). Permutations actually account for which specific sevens. In other words, that first 7 7 X combination could be 7♥ 7♠ X, 7♥ 7♣ X, 7♥ 7♦ X, 7♠ 7♥ X, 7♠ 7♣ X, 7♠ 7♦ X, 7♣ 7♥ X, 7♣ 7♠ X, 7♣ 7♦ X, 7♦ 7♥ X, 7♦ 7♠ X, or 7♦ 7♣ X—and likewise for the other two combinations! Needless to say, the total number of permutations (36) is greater, since it takes into account more factors (here, both rank and suit). Of course, a three-card poker player has no reason to care what suits the sevens are, just that they form a pair. But in other games and situations, that player would want to consider both the way things might be grouped and what type they are.

The Payout

One way the house (casino) gains an edge is by paying out a bet at less than the real odds. To get a quick sense of this, imagine that someone flipping a coin requests that you give him $5 for the chance to win $3. You'd quickly dismiss such an offer, since the reward simply isn't worth the risk! That's similar to how the games in the casino work. You essentially risk more than you have a chance of winning back.

For instance, an American roulette wheel has thirty-eight different numbers (1 to 36, plus 0 and 00).

Therefore, the chance of any one number coming up is 1 in 38, or 37 to 1. But most casinos only pay 35 to 1. That built-in discrepancy—the cause of the term "negative expectation"—means you'll tend to lose money in the long run even if your winning number comes up a relatively "normal" number of times.

Consider a "perfect" set of spins. Theoretically (but not often in real life), every thirty-eight spins would see each number come up once. Thus, if you wagered $1 on the same number for all thirty-eight spins, one time you'd win $35 and get to keep your $1 bet. So you'd have wagered $38 and be left with $36. That means for every $38 you wager, the house gladly keeps the $2 difference. Since $\frac{2}{38}$ equals 0.0526, the house advantage is said to be 5.26%—which, as you'll see, is not very good for the player.

Another way to measure the risk vs. reward of a bet is by multiplying the chance of winning a bet by how much you could win and subtracting the chance of losing multiplied by how much you would lose. Recycling the above example, you have a 1 in 38 chance of winning $35 and a 37 in 38 chance of losing $1. Mathematically, that's ($\frac{1}{38}$ x 35) – ($\frac{37}{38}$ x 1), which equals 0.9211 – 0.9737, for a difference of –0.0526. In other words, 5.26% against the player (and for the casino),

It's possible to determine that a bet with a 5.26% house advantage isn't such a great proposition from experience. Before losing money to simply test a theory (essentially what gambling is, when you break it down), it's more practical to first take a look around at other house advantages in other games and compare. Craps is a good example. That game has several bets that are better and several that are worse. In fact, a couple of the simplest, most popular bets have a house advantage of 1.41% and 16.67%. Suddenly 5.26% doesn't seem so bad—or so good.

just like we figured above. If a computation like that yielded a positive number, it would indicate a bet that's good for the player. Unfortunately, it doesn't come out positive as often as players would like!

What It Means

The house advantage isn't the chance of winning the bet. It's a measure of how much a player stands to lose in the long run by making a particular bet. For instance, a particular bet might have a 47% chance of winning, but a 5.26% house advantage. That means that for every $100 put into play, the player can expect to lose $5.26. Not within a few spins, but over hundreds of spins.

The Law of Averages

If you see a roulette wheel hit red seven times in a row, do you think you should bet red because it's "hot" or black because it's "due"? There's no right answer to this rhetorical question. It's just to point out a common misconception around the casino. Red has the same chance of coming up on any spin of the wheel, no matter what the history. Statistically, a tossed coin has the same chance of coming up heads ten times in a row as it does five heads and five tails or every other one—or any random pattern, for that matter. Consider the classic example of an infinite number of monkeys at typewriters eventually producing Shakespeare's plays. Imagine how many of them were only off by a few words! The point is that it's easy to get drawn in to the psychology, but you should be careful about assuming anything is "supposed" to happen in the casino. Some things are more likely than others, but that doesn't mean they have to happen. If that were the case, events within games would be predictable and the casinos wouldn't last very long!

And it doesn't even matter if it's the same player betting during those hundreds of spins. All the casino cares about is that money is in play. With a built-in house advantage on every game, all the money played among all the various games over thousands of plays adds up to millions of dollars in revenue for the casino. That means you, the player, need to be conscious of not only what bets you're making, but the speed at which you're making them and how much overall time you're spending at the tables. Of course, that's in addition to keeping track of whether you're up or down for each session of play!

"Luck sometimes visits a fool, but never sits down with him."

—*Danish proverb*

Each game has its own rules and rituals about what players should do and how they should act. But there are certain conventions of common sense and common courtesy that prevail throughout. Ultimately, casino patrons aren't expected to be perfect angels, but we should at least act with a certain amount of dignity and self-respect.

Attire

Some places are nicer than others, but if you plan to be taken seriously anywhere, dress the part. Tuxedos aside, this at least means avoiding looking like you're on your way to or from the pool. Comfort and style are fine, but the casino floor is no place for swimsuits, tank tops, and flip-flops.

The Rules

Rules for the same games may differ slightly (or not so slightly) in different casinos. After reading this book, you'll know more about what questions to ask. Dealers will try to answer your questions as best they can, but try to get your questions about how to play answered before you sit down. Any pit boss (the floor supervisor) will be happy to provide you with a written copy of the rules for any game.

Getting Chips

Always put your money on the table. Dealers aren't allowed to take it from your hands.

How Much to Bet

Each table game has a plaque indicating the minimum and maximum bets. These change based on the casino and time of day. Be aware of them before you sit down at the table and as you play. Otherwise it slows down the game for everyone else.

How to Bet

In most games (especially card games), you're given your own space to place bets. But in games like roulette, you might share a space with other players. Do your best not to reach over and around other players. If you can't reach the proper area, ask the dealer to place the bet for you. If the game offers chairs, you most likely need to be sitting in one of them in order to play.

Your Cards

In games like blackjack, where all the players' cards are faceup, never touch your cards. In games like poker, where the players' cards are (at least partially) hidden, don't discuss your hand or that of any other player.

Not Your Chips

Never touch another player's chips or money.

Not Your Business

Even if another player asks for advice on a particular bet, don't give it. You have enough to worry about without worrying about another player losing their money from your advice!

The Dealers

Be respectful. They're trying to do a job. They don't want you to lose your money any more than you do. So don't accuse, swear at, or otherwise abuse them. And on the opposite side of the spectrum, don't chat them up the whole time you're at the table. They're there to run the game, not be your best buddy. Try to strike a balance by being polite, friendly, and not overly talkative. And especially if you like the service they're providing, be sure to "toke" (tip) them.

Winning

Again, it varies, but as a rule, don't grab at your chips as soon as you're paid off on a particular win. As tempting as that is, it's better to wait until everyone for that hand or spin is paid off before collecting your earnings. You'll want to do this at the right time so that the money isn't considered a parlay (a combined bet for the next hand or spin).

Enjoy Yourself

Feel free to enjoy a beverage—it's part of the fun, just as long as you don't overdo it. And remember to tip the waitress—$1 chips are fine.

Casinos have gotten friendlier over the past several decades. This is most likely as a result of the fact that their patrons have more and more choices as to where to give their business. So please do your part to uphold that friendly atmosphere while trying to have a good time.

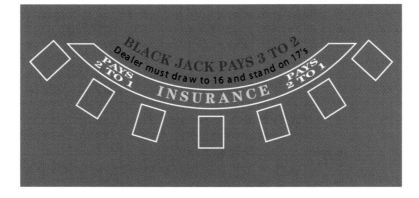

BLACKJACK

"Luck? Sure. But only after long practice and only with the ability to think under pressure."
—Babe Didrikson Zaharias (1914–1956), U.S. sportswoman

The Cards	Their Values
Aces	Either 1 or 11
2s through 10s	Face value
Jacks, queens, and kings	10 (These three face cards, along with actual tens, will be referred to throughout as "10s.")

Blackjack has been the most popular table game for the past four decades, in large part due to a college professor named Edward Thorp. In 1962, Thorp's book *Beat the Dealer* showed the game's optimal mathematical strategy. He showed how, based on the rules of blackjack, players have only one statistically valid play in any situation. It won't always produce a winning result—and making the "wrong" play might win every now and again. But over the long run, players who stick to Thorp's basic strategy can significantly cut the house advantage from 2% or 3% down to about 0.5%.

If blackjack offers such good odds, then why does it tend to be the second-highest source of revenue for casinos after slots? It has potentially good odds, so a lot of people play to try to "beat the house" or make mistakes in basic strategy, either through ignorance or just plain error. Because so many people play, all those errors add up and the casinos make a lot of money. It

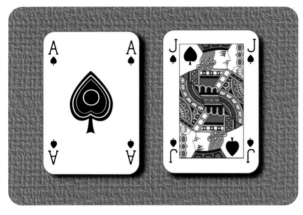

A natural

makes players want to try to beat the house, but it's a vicious circle! And it also explains why the casinos make so many blackjack tables available for play.

Blackjack tables typically offer a layout similar to the one shown on page 34. The seats farthest to the right and left are called "first base" and "third base," respectively. Since first base is first to make a decision, you'll probably want to sit closer to third base when you're just learning to play. Likewise, you'll probably want to look for a table with a relatively low minimum bet, such as $5.

Before any cards are dealt, players wishing to play must place their wagers in the betting area (usually a circle or casino logo) in front of where they're seated. The dealer deals each player two cards faceup and herself one up and one down.

An ace and any 10 on the first two cards
totals 21, forming a "blackjack" or "natural."

If the dealer's up card is an ace, she will invite players
to take "insurance." This is a side bet of up to half the
player's original bet that the dealer has a 10 in the hole
(facedown) for a blackjack. If the dealer doesn't have a
blackjack, insurance bets immediately lose and the
hand continues as normal. If the dealer does have a
blackjack, insurance bets win, paying 2 to 1. (Since the
wager was up to half, a win could equal the original
bet.) However, all the original bets lose—except for any
player blackjacks, which "push" (tie). Thus, for the most
part, hedging against a dealer blackjack with insurance
is a chance to break even. But despite the number of
tens in the deck, insurance bets tend to lose more than
they win. Bottom line: don't take insurance.

If a player has a blackjack and the dealer doesn't,
he is immediately paid winnings of 3 to 2 (1½ times
the bet). After paying out any blackjacks, the dealer
asks the player at first base (or the first to her left not
to have a blackjack) if he wants another card. The player
either indicates with a side-to-side hand gesture that
he'd like to stay (get no more cards) or with a scratching
gesture that he'd like to hit (get another card). See the

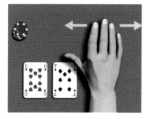

Stay (no more cards)

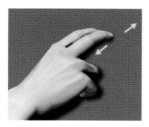

Hit (get another card)

figures at left for examples of how to do this.

> These gestures are very important, since they clearly state your intentions to both the dealer and the "eyes in the sky"—security cameras trained on the table to make sure play goes smoothly.

The player may continue to take additional cards, but if his hand busts (totals more than 21), he automatically loses. Eventually the player stays or busts (hopefully the former) and the dealer moves to the next player clockwise. After all the players have been given a chance to improve their hands with additional cards, the dealer turns over her down card and—as is usually indicated on the table—draws additional cards until her total is 17 or higher.

If in the process the dealer busts, she pays even money (matching the original bets) to each player without a blackjack who didn't bust. If the dealer's hand totals between 17 and 21, she takes the wagered chips of each losing player whose total is lower than hers and pays even money to each winning player whose total is higher than hers. Winners take back their winnings and their original bets. All players who want to play in the next hand then have to place their next bets in the betting area.

One of the biggest misconceptions surrounding blackjack is that the goal is to try to get a total as close as possible to 21. It's easy to see where this misunderstanding comes from, since the game is commonly known as "twenty-one" (a direct translation from its original French name, *vingt-et-un*). While getting a total of 18 to 21 is very good, the real goal for players is to reach a reasonably solid total and then wait for the dealer to bust. This is entirely the point behind basic strategy, which gives players a logical move for any two-card total against a particular dealer up card.

> No matter what the dealer's up card, assume the down card is a 10. Thus, if the dealer shows a 7, assume she has a total of 17. The dealer may or may not in fact have a 10 in the hole; but since four out of the thirteen ranks in the deck have a value of 10, it would be her most likely total.

Basic strategy for blackjack is based on the mathematical analysis of every possible outcome for the draw of cards and can be summarized with the following guidelines:

Stay on hard 17 through 21. You're more likely to bust than improve your hand!

Hard Total

"Hard total" means the total of the cards is fixed—there's no other way to add up the cards (such as an ace being counted as 1 or 11).

Hard 17 through hard 21

For hard 13 through 16, stay if the dealer's up card is a 6 or lower; otherwise, hit. Again, you're assuming the dealer's hole card is a 10 and you know the dealer has to stay on 17 or greater. Thus it makes sense to wait on a 6 or lower to bust, but not a 7 or higher.

With a hard 12, stay against a dealer's up card of 4 through 6; otherwise, hit. You stay to give the dealer a chance to bust before you. And you hit because if the dealer doesn't bust, then you'll lose.

An 11 is a player's second-favorite total (after 21). Double down unless the dealer shows an ace. You still have a decent possibility of catching a 21, but it's not worth the extra risk against the dealer's strongest up card.

With the first two cards totaling 10, double down if the dealer's up card is less than a 10. If it's a 10 or ace, just hit. Those are strong dealer cards, so you don't want to chance getting only one more card that might not help you.

If your hand totals 9, double down if the dealer's up card is a 3 through 6; otherwise, just hit. You can't bust, but the dealer is fairly likely to.

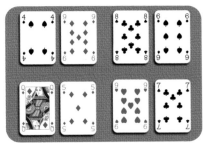

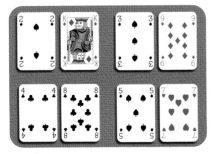

Hard 13 through hard 16

Hard 12

Hard 10

Hard 11

Doubling Down

Doubling down is something a player with a strong two-card total does when the dealer has a weak-looking up card. The player matches his original bet (see figure on left) in an effort to take advantage of the dealer's potential vulnerability to busting. In return, the dealer deals the player one final card, usually sideways across the first two.

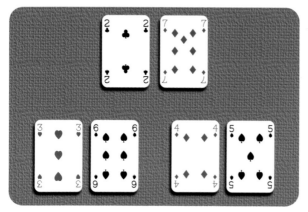

Hard 9

Any time that your hand totals between 5 and 8, then hit. Since you can't bust, another card can only help you.

For a soft 13 or 14, double down if the dealer shows a 5 or 6; otherwise, just hit. As 15 and 16 (the presumed dealer totals) are the highest totals at which the dealer must take another card, they're the most likely to bust.

With a soft 15 and 16, double down if the dealer shows a 4 through 6; otherwise, just hit. At least nine

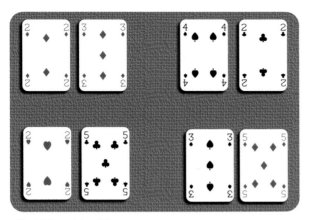

Hard 5 through hard 8

Soft Total

"Soft total" means an ace gives the total some flexibility. An ace and a 6 makes a soft 17, since it could be worth either 7 or 17 (depending on the value assigned the ace). It's treated differently from a hard total, since it's impossible to bust by adding a card to a soft total.

cards could improve your hand and the dealer is still likely to bust.

On a soft 17, double down against a dealer showing a 3 through 6; otherwise, just hit. Every card either helps

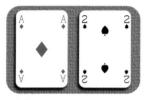

Soft 13

Soft 14

Soft 15

Soft 16

Soft 17

Soft 18

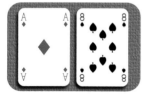

Soft 19

Soft 20

your hand, doesn't affect it, or makes it a hard total at which you'd stay anyway. It never makes sense to stay with this hand.

With a soft 18, also double down against a dealer showing a 3 through 6. But stay on a 2, 7, or 8 and hit on a 9, 10, or ace. This is probably the trickiest one to remember—and explain!

With a soft 19 or 20, stay nice and easy, as these are very strong hands that are not worth messing with!

Always split aces and 8s. The 8s because 16 is an undesirable total and the two hands could each become 18, and the aces because 12 isn't very strong, but a majority of

Splitting

Splitting is an optional move the player can do when dealt a pair. If the player matches his original bet by placing additional chips up to the same value in the betting area, the dealer will break the cards into two hands, add an up card to each, and allow them to be played out separately.

cards will help each ace to make a good hand. After aces are split, they only receive one other card, but every other split hand can receive more— and can be resplit if the

Always split aces and 8s.

first card pairs up again (usually until you have a maximum of four hands at the same time) and/or double down if one of the split hands produces a strong total.

Never split 10s (or any combination of 10s, jacks, queens, and kings)—always stay. Twenty is a great total and is definitely not something you want to risk destroying.

Split 9s against almost everything, staying only against a 7, 10, or ace. The 10 and ace are too strong

Surrendering

Surrendering is a sort of mercy rule for players. It gives them the option to forfeit a hand that's unlikely to win against a strong dealer up card in return for half their original bet back. There are two versions, early surrender and late surrender, both of which give the player an advantage. Early surrender was started in Atlantic City and means you can give up before the dealer checks for blackjack. Late surrender means that the dealer checks first for blackjack and doesn't offer a surrender if she has it.

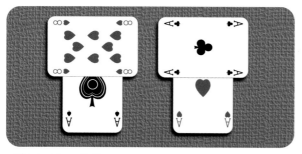

After aces are split, they can only receive one other card.

and an unsplit 18 beats (the presumed) 17.

Split 7s, 3s, and 2s against a dealer up card of 7 or less; otherwise, hit. In the case of the 7s, split because 14 is a weak total. The 3s and 2s are likely to produce a similarly weak total with the next hit.

Split 6s when the dealer shows a 6 or lower; otherwise, hit. You don't want to get two hands totaling 16, but if the dealer is weak, it's better to have two hands than one. Never split 5s—just treat them like

A Few Random Facts:

• Blackjack is 21, but 21 (which may have more cards) isn't necessarily blackjack.

• A 21 from split aces may not be treated as a blackjack.

• The dealer may assume you'll want to stick on certain totals, but will never give you another card unless you ask for it.

• It's possible to play multiple hands at once, as long as you're quick enough to make all those decisions!

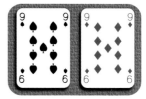

Split 9s against everything but a 7, 10, or ace.

Split 7s against a dealer up card of 7 or less.

Split 6s when the dealer shows a 6 or lower.

Only split 4s against a dealer's 5 or 6.

any other hand totaling 10. Only split 4s against a dealer's 5 or 6; otherwise, hit. Again, you are hoping to capitalize on a likely dealer bust hand.

That's a lot of rules for something called basic strategy! The bad news is that it only gets more complicated, based on one of the other big fallacies: blackjack is always played with the same rules each time. In fact, this is far from the truth.

These guidelines are based on certain rules that many casinos use, specifically:

• Multiple decks are used.

• The dealer stays on all 17s (hard and soft).

• Players can double down on any two cards (not just totals of 10 and/or 11).

• It's possible to double down after a split.

• Surrender isn't offered.

An example of when you might surrender is if you had a hard 15 against a dealer 10 or a hard 16 against a dealer's up card being a 9, 10, or ace. That's the simplified version, but the point is that totals of 15 and 16 are likely to bust, and even if they don't, they're likely to win against those dealer up cards less than half the time. Surrender can usually only be done on the first two cards and is unique in the sense that it's the only option that you indicate verbally (rather than with a gesture).

Using multiple decks is bad for the player, but all the other options listed on the opposite page are good. You want to be able to split and double down as much as possible. If you're not allowed to double down on any two cards, in most cases you want to take a hit. But with soft 18, you want to stay. You don't want the dealer to have to hit on soft 17! Be sure to ask the dealer or pit boss about these rules.

You may see other versions of blackjack with various gimmicks such as "mad 21," "super 7s," and "no bust 21." They're not all bad. For instance, Spanish 21 offers pretty good odds, but uses a very different strategy (known as the "Armada") for optimal play based on several bonuses.

Doubling down after a split

"As long as we are lucky we attribute it to our smartness; our bad luck we give the gods credit for."

—*Josh Billings (1818–1885), U.S. writer*

ROULETTE

American wheel

Roulette has been a casino gambling icon for hundreds of years. Two versions of the wheel survive to this day, both of which originated in France and feature thirty-six red and black pockets. The "American" wheel appeared in Paris in the late eighteenth century and gained popularity in New Orleans in the early nineteenth century, and has two green pockets (0 and 00). The "French" or "European" wheel was introduced in Monaco in the mid-nineteenth century, and features only one green pocket (0).

French or European wheel

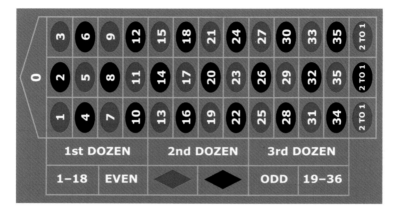

French table layout

Although the single-zero version offers the player slightly better odds, either format is just as easy to play. Each offers a bounty of potential rewards with every mesmerizing spin of the wheel. There's just something so alluring about watching a small white ball bounce around randomly, hoping it happens to land in a pocket that favors your bet(s).

Speaking of which, the French and American table layouts both offer quite a variety of bets. With a single chip, it's possible to bet on one, two, three, four, five, six, twelve, or eighteen numbers at once. Notice that except for the five-number bet, all of the others multiply evenly into thirty-six. This isn't by accident. In fact, nothing about the table layout is. For example, each of

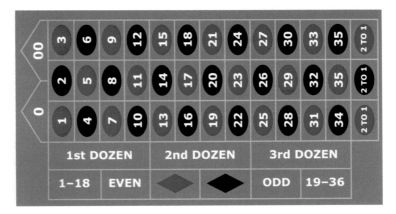

American table layout

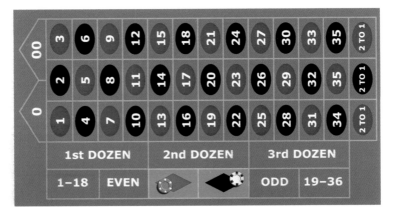

The red or black even-money bet

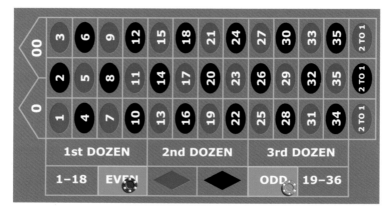

Even and odd bets

the dozens (1–12, 13–24, 25–36) has six reds and six blacks. And each of the halves (1–18, 19–36) has nine reds and nine blacks. It's a very balanced, purposeful setup, right down to the payouts offered on each bet.

Roulette offers three popular even-money bets: red or black, odd or even, and 1–18 or 19–36. They're said to be that way because they pay even money (1 to 1), not because they're an even proposition. Remember, including the two zeros, the wheel has thirty-eight numbers. Each even bet covers eighteen numbers— that's less than half of the numbers. In fact, you may be surprised to find out that despite covering more numbers, a bet on red or black gives up the same house advantage as betting on any single number!

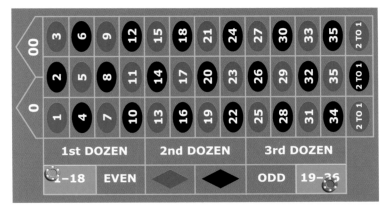

1–18 and 19–36 bets

Again, that doesn't mean the two bets have the same chance of winning each spin. It means that over time, with dozens of spins, you're just as likely to lose the same amount of money on either bet.

In thirty-eight perfect spins, betting $1 on red every time, you would win $1 eighteen times. You'd also get to keep your $1 bet, leaving you with $36. Subtracting that $36 you won from the $38 you wagered leaves the casino with a $2 profit. Dividing $2 by the total amount wagered ($38) yields a 5.26% house advantage. This is the same figure that we calculated for betting on a single number on page 25! As it turns out—are you sitting down?—all but one of the bets described below offer that same exact house advantage in the long run.

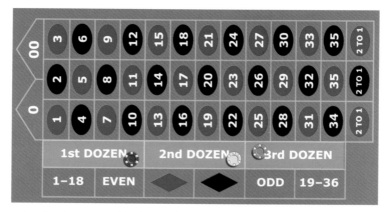

To make a bet on one of the dozens, place a chip in one of the "dozens" areas.

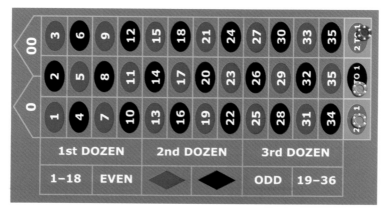

To make a bet on the other dozens, put a chip at the foot of one of the columns.

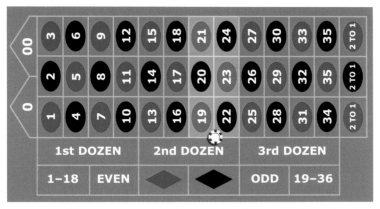

To make a "line" bet, place a chip at the intersection of two rows and one of the dozens.

A twelve-number bet on one of the dozens or columns pays 2 to 1. To make this bet, simply place your chips in one of the "dozens" areas or at the foot of one of the columns.

A six-number (also known as a "line") bet pays 5 to 1. To make this bet, place your chips at the intersection where two rows cross with one of the dozens areas (as shown above).

A four-number "corner" or "square" bet pays 8 to 1. Just place your chips at a four-way intersection of numbers.

A three-number "street" bet has an 11 to 1 payoff. Position your chips at the intersection of the row with

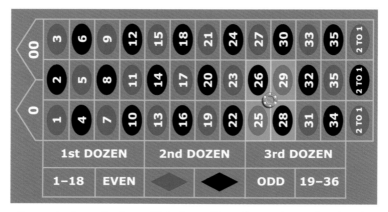

Four-number "corner" or "square" bet: place a chip at a four-way intersection of numbers.

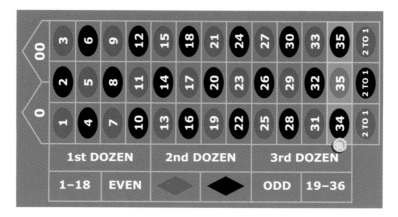

For a "street" bet, place a chip at the intersection of the row with one of the dozens.

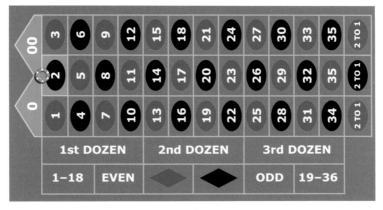

Three-number bet, covering the 0, 00, and 2

one of the dozens. There is another kind of three-number bet with the same payout, involving covering the 0, 00, and 2 with the chip.

A two-number "split" bet has a 17 to 1 payoff. To go for this bet, put your chips at the border between any two numbers.

And as discussed earlier, a one-number "straight" bet has a 35 to 1 payoff. Your chips go right in the middle of any one number. If another player puts chips on the number you want, just place your chips right on top. (You don't want it to be confused with a corner or split bet.) In fact, that goes for any of the "inside" bets (involving the thirty-eight actual numbers). Each player's chips are of a different color, so there is no confusion.

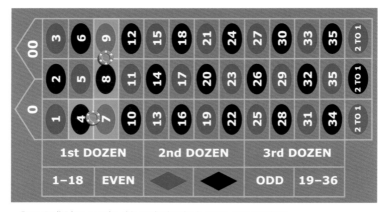

For a "split" bet, put the chip at the border between two numbers.

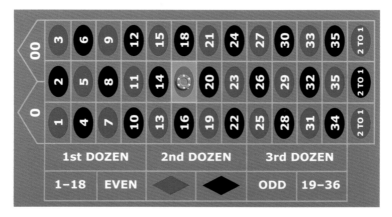

A "straight" bet goes right on top of the number.

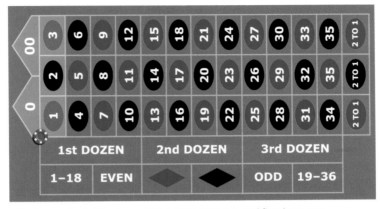

The five-number bet involves putting a chip on the 0, 1, and first dozen area.

If you ever forget a payout ratio for a bet, don't worry about it. All you need to remember is the number 36. To figure out any bet's payout, just divide how many numbers are covered by the bet into 36, then subtract one. For instance, a street bet covers three numbers. Three into 36 is 12, and minus one is 11. As mentioned above, the street bet pays 11 to 1.

The five-number bet is the oddball. It seems like a good bet because it covers 0, 00, 1, 2, and 3. It's made by putting chips on the intersection of the 0, 1, and first dozen areas. However, it doesn't multiply evenly into 36. The 6 to 1 payout leaves you with a whopping 7.89% house advantage—that is not particularly good!

As for all the other roulette bets, they have the same 5.26% house advantage—it doesn't matter how you combine them. For instance, you could bet $1 on even and $1 on black. It might seem like you'd increase your odds by covering twenty-six numbers at once (ten of which are both even and black), but you wouldn't. In thirty-eight perfect spins, you'd win $1 thirty-six times (eighteen for all the even numbers and another eighteen for the black ones). You'd also keep your original $1 bet those thirty-six times, leaving you with $72. But since you were betting $2 per spin, that's $76 you wagered. Take the difference between what you wagered and what you won ($4) and divide by the total amount wagered ($76) and you wind up with a house advantage of . . . 5.26%!

Roulette does offer ways to play with better odds—primarily with the single-zero wheel. As mentioned before, these are used throughout Europe. But they're also used around the world in Australia, Canada, and even the United States. That includes casinos in Atlantic City, the South, and Las Vegas. In the United States, these wheels might only be in the high-roller areas or have large minimum bets. Anywhere you find one, eliminating that 00 cuts the house edge almost in half, to 2.7%.

Another rule that cuts the edge is called *en prison* (usually found in European casinos). It works with any of the even bets (red/black, etc.). Let's say you've bet black and the 0 comes up. With this rule, instead of losing right away, the bet is held (literally, "in prison") until the next spin. If that next spin is black, you get your bet back (and don't win anything on it). If it's not black, you lose it. In American casinos, this is known as "surrender." On either type of wheel, it cuts the house advantage in half (2.63% American, 1.35% European) for those bets. At 1.35%, it's no wonder roulette is so popular in Europe!

Because Europeans play it so often, they have one more popular feature that isn't so common in the United States: "announce" or "call" bets. Most often, these refer to "neighbors"—or *voisons*, as the French say—on the wheel. For instance, *voisons du zero* (also called "zero's neighbors" or "series 0/2/3") refers to a group of seventeen numbers in and around the 0 pocket and is made as a combination of different types of bets on the layout with multiples of nine chips. Similarly, *tier du cylindre* (or "series 5/8") covers twelve particular numbers opposite 0 on the wheel with a series of six split bets. *Orphelins à cheval* represents eight numbers with a combination of straight and split

A Few General Pointers for Roulette:

• When you change in your money for chips, the chip value is assumed to be $1 unless you specify another denomination.

• Never lean over the wheel.

• Pay attention to when the dealer says "No more bets."

• Don't grab your winnings until the dealer removes the win marker (usually the size of a chess piece).

• If you're looking for a bet as easy as red/black in the United States, but with better odds, either of the two main bets in mini baccarat are a good place to start.

bets in multiples of five units, while *orphelins à plein* covers those same eight numbers with eight straight bets. Other special bets cover series of numbers that end in certain digits. And a more generic neighbor bet can be made by calling out that you want a certain number and so many of its neighbors (on either side of the pocket).

BIG SIX / WHEEL OF FORTUNE

The American wheel

Ancient Greek soldiers invented a game based on marking sections of their shields, spinning the shields atop spears, and betting where the sections would stop. Romans played similar games by spinning chariot wheels and using the spokes. In more recent times, carnival barkers at fairgrounds have spun large, colorful, vertical wheels and challenged patrons to guess on which number the wheels would stop. The modern casino version of this folly is known as "big six" or "wheel of fortune."

The "six" refers to the number of possible bets; the "fortune" is what the casinos tend to make from people foolish enough to play the game! (You may remember it as the only game in the movie *Rain Man* at which Dustin Hoffman's character lost.)

Playing is simple enough: Put your money down on any of the six different numbers or symbols on the table layout. These numbers and symbols correspond directly to spaces on the wheel. When the bets are down, the dealer announces "No more bets" and gives the wheel a whirl. If the indicator stops the wheel on the number or symbol you bet on, you win.

Like roulette, the wheel comes in two international flavors. The American version has fifty-four spaces, often inlaid with actual bills. Each bill denomination

Space	Number of Spaces	House Advantage
$1	24	11.11%
$2	15	16.67%
$5	7	22.22%
$10	4	18.52%
$20	2	22.22%
Joker/Logo	2	24.07% (at 40 to 1) or 14.81% (at 45 to 1)

indicates the payout ratio. In other words, a bet on $1 pays 1 to 1, $2 pays 2 to 1, $5 pays 5 to 1, etc. The spaces marked by a joker or the casino's logo generally pay 40 to 1—sometimes 45 to 1 in Atlantic City and some other locales. Now the bad news—all of these payouts work against the player (see above).

The Australian version of the money wheel is a little better. Its fifty-two spaces offer denominations of $1, $3, $5, $11, and $23, with a 47 to 1 payout on the joker/logo. This works out to an overwhelming 7.69% house advantage.

It's an easy game to play, but no amount of skill can compensate for the high house edge. Even covering multiple numbers wouldn't help. In fact, let's look at the case where a player covers every number with a $1 bet, just to drive home the point.

In fifty-four perfect spins, where each space on the wheel is hit once, the player would win $24 on the twenty-four $1 bets, $30 on the fifteen $2 bets, $35 on the seven $5 bets, $40 on the four $10 bets, $40 on the two $20 bets, and $80 on the joker/logo bets (each at 40 to 1), adding up to $249. Plus, the player would keep the one $1 bet that won each of the fifty-four spins, for another $54. This gives the player a theoretical grand total of $303. However, the player would have wagered $324 (54 x $6). Thus, the casino still has an advantage!

With horrendous odds like these, it's no wonder big six is outlawed in some states. The only possible reason to play this lousy game would be to take one spin for fun or if you can find a casino that offers a coupon for a 2 to 1 payout on a $1 bet.

"All of us have bad luck and good luck. The man who persists through the bad luck—who keeps right on going—is the man who is there when the good luck comes—and is ready to receive it."

—Robert Collier (1885–1950) U.S. author

CRAPS

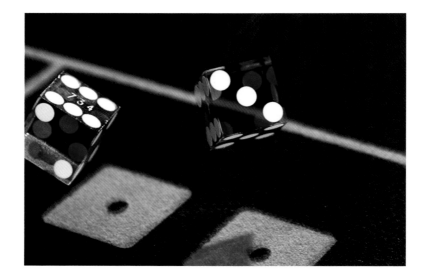

For thousands of years, people have rolled dice of clay, stone, wood, and even bone. Care to hazard a guess as to where the name "craps" came from? Actually, the answers are in the previous sentence. It's said that as

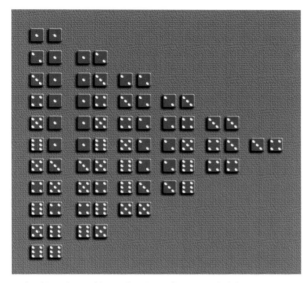

The thirty-six possible combinations of two six-sided dice

early as the 1100s, the English played a complex dice
game called hazard. The French adapted the game in
the 1700s and brought it to New Orleans in the 1800s,
where it underwent another transformation. In case
you're curious, the game's name comes from a
corruption of *krabs*, the French slang term for a pair of
ones. Craps gained increasing popularity through World
War II and to this day is second in casino popularity only
to blackjack.

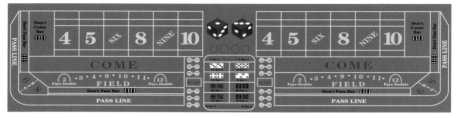

Table layout for craps

The reason for its wide appeal is that craps offers many different bets, lots of fun jargon, fast action, and some of the best odds in the house. However, it also offers some of the worst odds, potentially making it both the most exciting and misunderstood game in the casino.

Before getting into how to play, it's important to take a quick look at the numbers behind the game. The picture on page 71 shows the thirty-six different possible combinations that can be made with a pair of six-sided dice. From top to bottom, each row shows the different ways the totals two through twelve can be made. As you can see, seven has the most possible combinations (six), since each side of each die can be added to make a seven. This makes seven a very important facet of craps.

Next, we move to the table layout (as seen above). The players stand behind where it says "pass line." With up to eight on each side, as many as sixteen people can play at once. This is why the layout is repeated—every player has an area to stand and place their bets. If a section of the wooden rail around the top of the table doesn't have any chips in it, that means it's an open spot to stand, put your chips in, and play.

At the middle/bottom of the table is where a dealer, known as the "stickman," stands. He wrangles the dice for each shooter with a long, curved stick, calls out the dice totals as they appear, and helps the other dealers place some of the players' bets in the center. Opposite him sits the boxman (the only person sitting). This person puts the players' cash in the box in exchange for chips and generally presides over the action at the table. On either side of the boxman are two dealers. They help players on each side of the table place and collect their bets. In order to keep the game moving along quickly, these dealers have to be the best chip-handlers and the fastest number-crunchers in the casino.

As for the dice themselves, the ones you'll find in most casinos are ¾-inch red cubes made from translucent cellulose with white dots painted on. Casinos use tiny serial numbers to be able to quickly confirm any die being used is theirs. In order to run an honest game, each die used must have an exactly

equal chance of coming up any of the six numbers.
Thus, rule number one is that the shooter must always
keep both dice in plain view. That means:

> • Use one empty hand to pick them up (the
> mirrors around the inside of the table are to
> ensure it's an empty hand).

> • Never bring them outside the cylinder of the
> table.

> • Never hold them with two hands, switch the
> dice between hands, or blow on them.

The bottom line is that players shouldn't do anything
that might give the impression that they're introducing
outside dice (especially ones that are "loaded," or
weighted for certain numbers to appear more often
than others) into the game. It's okay to shake the dice
in your hand, but it's better to just pick them up with
your fingertips.

Each player around the table will be given a chance
to roll the dice. When rolling the dice, it's important to
toss them the length of the table. In order to be a legal
roll, both dice must bounce off the egg crate–shaped
foam back wall. This effectively randomizes each roll. It's
not necessary to throw the dice hard. Just make sure
they get to the end of the table with a light toss. They

shouldn't be bouncing around, knocking bets over and springing off the table, but accidents do happen. If a die comes off the table near you (as a player or spectator), just pick it up and hand it to one of the dealers. They'll hand it to the boxman, who will inspect it, make sure it's the same die that left the table, and get the shooter another die to continue the roll. (Some shooters are superstitious and specifically request the same die that left the table.)

Okay, now that you know a little about the table, personnel, and equipment, you're almost ready to bet—you just need chips. As with all games, you need to put your bills on the table. Don't worry about the bills being confused for a bet. A dealer will get the money to the boxman, who'll count it out and authorize the dealer to give you that amount in chips. If the dealers are a little busy, you may need to wait a roll, but they'll take care of you.

The dealer may ask what denomination of chips you want or may just assume what you want and give them to you. You can always trade up or down later. For instance, if you get "greens" ($25 chips) and don't plan on betting that much at once, you can always slide them toward the dealer and ask for "reds" ($5 chips) in their place.

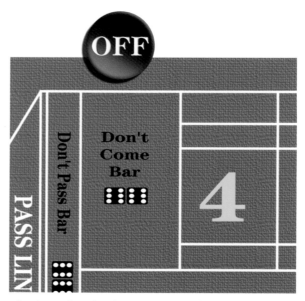

Bet the pass line when the puck indicates "off."

It's time for your first bet, so let's start with a good one. Place a chip (at least the table minimum) in the pass line area right in front of where you're standing. Pass line bets are done right before a shooter starts a new sequence, while the puck indicates "off" (on the black side with white letters). That means a shooter is about to make a "come out" roll. The stickman will push two dice (or five, from which two are chosen) to the player, who picks them up and rolls them.

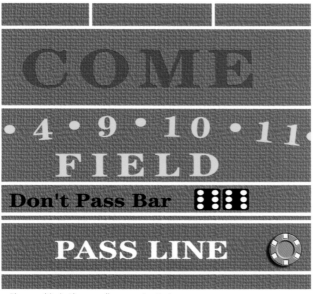

Place a chip in the pass line area to start.

If the dice total two, three, or twelve, that's a "craps." You immediately lose your pass line bet and replace it with another. If a seven or eleven is rolled, that's a "natural." You immediately win the bet at 1 to 1, pick up your winnings, and leave your original bet on the pass line. Otherwise, a "point number"—four, five, six, eight, nine, or ten—is established (also called just a "point" or "number"). The dealer will turn the puck to "on" (white) and place it in the point number's box.

Once a point number has been set, the puck indicates "on."

In order to win your pass line bet now, that number has to be rolled again before a seven comes up. Thus, if you walk up to a table and the puck is in the "six" box, right away you know that players are rooting for a six to be rolled. Once a point is established, craps and elevens aren't a factor. The only two totals that matter are the particular point number or a seven.

Since there are eight ways to make a seven or eleven (1-6, 2-5, 3-4, 4-3, 5-2, 6-1, 5-6, and 6-5) and only four

An odds bet

ways to make a two, three, or twelve (1-1, 1-2, 2-1, and 6-6), the chances of an instant win vs. loss on the come-out roll are 2 to 1. That's an advantage for the player. However, since there are more ways to make a seven than any other number, once a point is established, the player is at a disadvantage. So a seven can be good or bad, depending on the timing. (An eleven is never bad, only good or neutral.) What this adds up to (without getting into the actual figures) is pass line bets have an

For the Points	The Odds Are	(Simplified)
6 or 8	6 to 5	6 to 5
5 or 9	6 to 4	3 to 2
4 or 10	6 to 3	2 to 1

overall house advantage of only 1.41%. Very respectable—and they get better.

When a point is rolled, the casino gives the player an opportunity to do something unique: make the only bet in the house that pays true odds without a commission. Appropriately enough, it's called an "odds" bet. To take odds—also known as "free odds"—put up to the same amount as your pass line bet right behind the pass line. Now if the point repeats before the next seven, you'll get paid 1 to 1 on your pass line bet and true odds on your odds bet. In other words, the actual ratio of the number of ways to make a seven (six) against the number of ways to make each other number. The odds have been summed up in the table above.

If you bet $5 on the pass line and a six was rolled, you backed it up with a $5 odds bet, and a six appeared again before a seven, you'd get paid $5 for your pass line bet and $6 (6/5 x $5) for your odds bet. (Then you'd pick up your $21 in original bets and winnings and make another pass line bet.) By always adding odds bets to your pass line bets, you cut the house advantage almost in half, to 0.8%.

Almost all casinos take it a step further by offering players "multiple odds." Most often, 2X (two times, or double) odds. This means that your odds bet can be up to twice as big as your pass line bet. If in the above example you'd had double odds, you could've put $10 in odds behind the six. When it hit, you'd still have won $5 for the pass line, but this time you'd have won $12 (6/5 x $10) for the odds bet. By consistently playing double odds this way, the house advantage slims down to 0.6%. The higher the multiple of odds, the lower the house advantage. It's not uncommon to see 3X, 4X, and 5X—even up to 100X in some places! Why do casinos offer such a way to significantly cut their edge? Remember, odds bets are only made when a point number is established. Thus, it's when the strong possibility of rolling a seven makes both those bets the most vulnerable. Knowing this, many players don't take full advantage of the odds opportunity, even though failing to do so greatly handicaps them.

Another thing many craps players don't do well is size their bets properly. Consider the case where a five is rolled in a casino offering single (regular, or 1X) odds. To back up the $5 pass line bet, the player instinctively puts down $5. Why is this incorrect? Because the payout is 3 to 2, that means the casino would have to pay $7.50 for true odds on the bet. The casino doesn't want to mess around with coins, so they allow the player to bet the next highest even amount, in this case $6. That way, if the five hits, the player wins $5 on the pass line bet and $9 (3/2 x $6) on the odds bet. (If you hadn't raised your odds bet, you would've only been paid $7 on it, thus shortchanging yourself.) Most dealers will alert players to situations like this by reminding them to place an extra dollar on top of their single odds bets behind a five or nine. But there's a different way of sizing your bet that they may not alert you to.

In casinos offering double odds, a special situation can arise when the point is six or eight. Consider a pass line bet of $10. An eight is rolled and the player quickly puts $20 in odds behind it. This isn't wrong, but it's not as right as it could be. The casino will actually allow the player to put down $25 in odds in that situation. Why more than twice the pass line bet? Because it affords the player the chance to be paid back in the highest denomination of chips used on the pass line. In other words, if the eight repeats before a seven, the player wins $10 on the pass line bet and $30 (6/5 x $25) on the odds bet, both of which can be paid in $5 chips. Rather than dollars, think of the bets in terms of chip units. The player bets two units on the pass line and can then bet four units in odds. But (the payout ratio) 6/5 x 4 is 24/5 units. The next highest number of units divisible by five (for an even payout) is five units. And that five units amounts to $25.

If you're playing double odds, just remember that for every $10 on the pass line you can bet $25 in odds. That way you quickly know that on a $40 pass line bet with a point of six or eight, you can put down $100 in odds. (For four, five, nine, or ten, you could still only put down $80.) With a pass line bet not cleanly divisible by ten, another way to figure the "full" (best) odds bet is by doubling the number of units and then looking for the next multiple of five. So when betting three units ($15), that doubles to six and the next multiple of five is ten. Thus you're allowed to bet ten units ($50) in odds to back up three on the pass line. Using units is especially handy when dealing with higher chip denominations (e.g., $25 and $100).

Of course, a third way to do it is simply by asking the dealer when a point of six or eight comes up what the maximum odds bet is. Even though it's a vulnerable

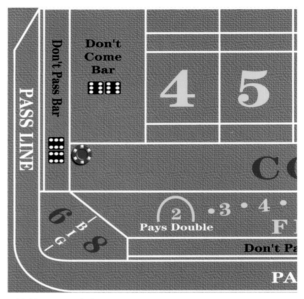

Making a come bet

bet because it pays at true odds, it gives players a special opportunity to lower the house advantage.

If the pass line were the only bet, craps would be a pretty good game, but a little boring. Think about it. On the come-out roll, the shooter establishes a point of nine. Out of the thirty-six possible rolls, that gives four (4-5, 5-4, 3-6, 6-3) that win, six (for any seven) that lose, and therefore twenty-six that don't affect it. Craps players like action, not standing around over two-thirds

Once a point is established, the dealer places the "come" bet in that box.

of the time. The "come" bet is similar to one on the pass line, but a come bet is made when a point is already established. It allows pass line bettors to have more than one number working for them at once. And new players can come to the table to join in the action when the puck is already "on."

To make a come bet, simply place chips in front of yourself in the come area. Just like with a pass line bet, a craps (two, three, or twelve) on the next roll loses; a

The dealer places the odds on a come bet, partially slid off.

natural (seven or eleven) wins; otherwise a point is established. This sets up an interesting give/take when a seven is rolled right after a come bet. For instance, let's say you have $10 on the pass line point of four with a $20 double odds bet behind it. You make a $10 come bet and a seven is rolled. You lose your $30 pass/odds bets, but win $10 on the come. So it's a sort of way of hedging your pass line bet against a seven. If instead of a seven, a three (or other craps) had appeared, you'd have lost the $10 come, but not affected the pass/odds. An eleven would've won the come and not affected the pass/odds. (You can see why players like elevens so much—that's why they yell "Yo-eleven!" when one is rolled.) If a point—say, nine—were rolled, the dealer would have taken your come bet and placed it in the nine box (see page 86). With multiple sets of chips in the box, how does the dealer know whose is whose? Where in the point number box the chips are placed relates to where around the table the corresponding players are standing. In this example, the player was probably standing to the stickman's far left.

Just like with pass line bets, players can (and should) place odds on come bets. The difference is that since the come bets are in the number boxes, the dealer actually puts the chips for the odds in the right place. With the number of bets flying around, this is where clear communication is especially important. Rather than just assuming the dealer knows what you want to do with the chips you place in front of him, specify that you want them to be "odds on the nine" (or whatever the point number). He'll put your odds on top of your come bet, partially slid off.

A common pass/come strategy is to have three numbers working at all times. In other words, you have

Making a place bet

a pass line bet with odds and two come bets with odds. Or just three come bets with odds (if you miss the come-out roll). Don't expect this to happen within the first three rolls every time. It might take several—or might not happen at all, if the dice don't cooperate. But when they do, three numbers is a good balance between covering a bunch of possible rolls and having too much money on the table that could be wiped out with a single seven. By the way, if the pass line number hits when you have other point numbers up, you're paid on the pass line bet and the other numbers remain. If the next (come-out) roll is a seven, you lose your other point number come bets but are returned the odds, since they're said to be "not working on the come-out" (again, you'll know because the puck will be "off").

Just as the dealer will pay your pass line winnings near the pass line, the dealer will also pay your come bet winnings in the come area. So it's important to stay focused on which numbers you have and when or where you're being paid. You never want to miss out! (Either someone else will gladly pick up your chips or the chips will stay in the come area and be assumed a bet for the next roll.) Once you get into a groove, you'll quickly figure out which chips the dealer is placing for you and which for other players, but it's still easy to get confused at a busy table, especially with all the potential activity on every roll from the different bets.

Of the six point numbers (four, five, six, eight, nine, ten), the six and eight have the highest chance of being rolled before a seven (as we've seen, 6 to 5). That makes them the most likely to come through on a pass or come bet. But some players don't want to wait for a six or eight to be rolled as a point, so they'll "place" those numbers whenever they feel like it. Of course, it comes at a premium. The casino won't just give you a great bet for nothing, so they pay out at less than true odds on place bets. For the six and eight, rather than 6 to 5, the payout is 7 to 6. Thus, you should always give the dealer $6, $12, or some multiple of six (so you can get paid evenly). The dealer will take your chips and put them just below the proper number box. The house advantage for placing the six or eight is a slender 1.52%. (It's possible to place the other numbers as well, but the house edge is a few times higher.)

One way to incorporate place numbers into your strategy would be to make a pass line bet. Place either the six or eight (based on which wasn't established as the point) and at the same time place a come bet (to protect against an immediate seven). At any time, you can call your place bets off. The dealer will place an "off" token on top of your chips and that bet won't be affected by any rolls until it is removed. Or you can take down the bet altogether—keep in mind that if you don't have the dealer take down the bet after a win, it may be assumed that you want to let it ride. Thus, the place bet is a reasonable, flexible bet. The biggest problem, however, is that you can't put odds on it.

Putting money on the "big six" or "big eight" is almost the same thing as placing those numbers.

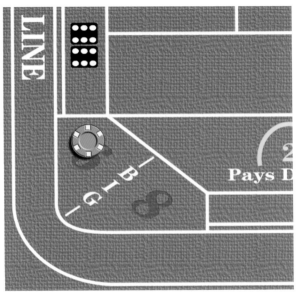

Putting money on the big six is foolish.

Actually, it's the same wager—that a six or an eight will appear before a seven—but it's only paid at even money. This weak payout gives the house a big 9.09% advantage. So, it's never a good idea to bet the big six or big eight.

"Buying" a number is a similar bet for those impatient types who want their money on a particular number immediately. The casino pays out true odds on these "buy" numbers, but it charges a 5% commission.

Buying the four

Because of the commission involved, buy bets are made in increments of $21—$1 of which is the built-in commission on the other $20. For the four or ten, that works out as a 4.76% house advantage. This is better than the 6.67% for placing either of them, but is still not good. And it wouldn't make sense to buy any of the other numbers, since it's possible to place any of them for a lower house advantage.

Up until now, the bets discussed (pass line, come, placing, buying) all have in common the fact that they're "right" bets. That doesn't mean they're correct, just that in betting "with the dice," you want other numbers to appear before a seven. But it's also possible to bet "against the dice," hoping that a seven appears before other numbers. This is also known as "wrong" betting, even though the odds can be very good.

The prime example of wrong betting is a bet on "don't pass." Since it's the exact opposite of a pass line bet, you immediately win on a two or three, lose on a seven or eleven, and on a point, you want to see a seven appear before that point repeats. The twelve is

A bet on don't pass

"barred" (meaning it's the only craps roll you don't win on the come-out) because otherwise the wrong bettor would actually have an edge over the house! This leaves the don't pass bettor at a disadvantage on the first roll, but at an advantage once a point is established. If a point does show up, the wrong bettor hopes for a four or ten, since they each only have three ways of being made and are therefore the most susceptible to a seven. The don't pass bet offers a minimal 1.4% house advantage, virtually the same as a pass line bet. The only difference is that you'll likely be rooting against what most of the other players want to see happen—so you may not want to cheer too loudly for that seven! Since it's not as popular, the don't pass area is smaller than the pass line. If you're going to bet wrong, you'll need to position yourself at the table in a way that makes that area easily accessible.

Just as with right odds bets, wrong odds bets are paid at true odds. But because a seven is more likely, the figures are flip-flopped. In other words, you'll get paid 1 to 2 on a winning four or ten, 2 to 3 on a five or nine,

The odds on a don't pass bet

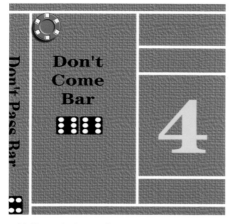

Making a don't come bet

and 5 to 6 on a six or eight. So you need to size your wrong odds bet to be divisible by two, three, or six, depending on which number is the point. For example, on the come-out roll you put $5 on don't pass and an eight is rolled. With single odds, you'd put $6 right on top of your don't pass bet. If a seven came up before an eight, everyone else would groan, but you'd collect $5 on your don't pass bet, as well as $5 on your odds bet. With double odds, you would have put $12 in odds and won $10.

"Don't come" works in much the same way. You place money in the proper area. If the come-out roll produces a point, the chips are moved to the proper box. You can then ask the dealer to put odds on the bet.

Just as impatient right bettors have options (placing and buying), so do wrong bettors: a "lay" bet, for example. Since there are only three ways to make either a four or a ten, they're the best ones to lay against. Tell the dealer you want to "lay the four" and the dealer will put your chips in the proper area (see diagram on page 96). Similar to figuring out the correct amount for wrong odds, sizing a lay bet takes some reverse thinking. For example, since a 5% commission is applied, $20 makes sense for a payout (yielding an even $1 commission); to get back $20 on a four or ten that pays 1 to 2, you'd have to bet $40. So, adding in the commission, you'd need to bet $41 to win $20. It's a lot of mental work, but the house advantage on laying a four or a ten is a somewhat reasonable 2.44%.

That pretty much takes care of any bets you'd want to even think about making. But just so you know what everything else on the table layout refers to . . .

A "field" bet (see diagram on page 96) is a bet that the next roll will be a two, three, four, nine, ten, eleven, or twelve. It pays even money except for "snake eyes" (a two) and "boxcars" (a twelve), which get paid either double or

The don't come bet is four.

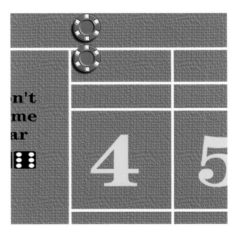

Odds on the don't come

Laying the four

Placing a field bet

triple the bet in various casinos. Depending on whether they pay double or triple, the overall house advantage for field bets is either 5.44% or 2.77%. It seems tempting because it's a bunch of numbers, but in reality it only covers sixteen out of the possible thirty-six rolls.

The rest of the "proposition" bets—or "props" for short—are in the center of the table. The first thing you'll notice is that the payouts are listed as "for," not "to." As we discussed earlier in the book, that means the casino takes your original bet and then pays you off at what seems like a higher rate when you win, rather than letting you keep your original bet and paying you at a lower rate.

Another sign that these should be avoided is the fact that the stickman will often encourage players to make these foolish bets, especially if a player has already done so. Some players out

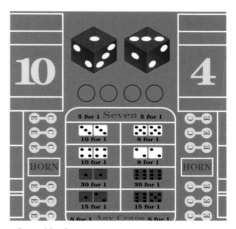

of habit, superstition, or ignorance continue to make these awful bets. That's why craps really is probably the worst game to learn from other players at the table, since many tend not to know what they are doing!

A bet on "any seven" seems like a good idea, since seven is such a popular roll. Six out of the thirty-six possible rolls are a seven, making it a 5 to 1 chance. But since the 5 for 1 payout is the equivalent of only 4 to 1, this bet has a 16.67% house advantage—the worst that craps has to offer!

The "any craps" bet (see diagram on page 98) has a similar dynamic to the any seven. Between two, three, and twelve, four out of the thirty-six rolls are covered, meaning that chances are 8 to 1 that a craps will appear. But the casino only pays 8 for 1, the equivalent of 7 to 1, which leaves them with an 11.11% advantage.

A bet on "C & E" (see diagram on page 98) is a bet on any craps or eleven

Proposition bets

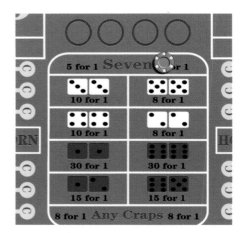

Any seven bet

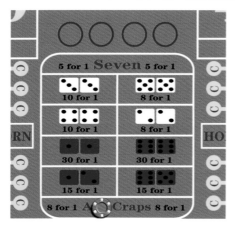

Any craps bet

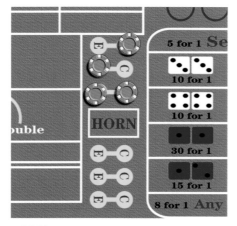

C & E bet

(5-6 or 6-5). Add any seven to the C & E bet and you've got the "world" bet. Both of these sound fun, but they have house edges that are over 10%.

Betting on the 1-1 or 6-6 seems exciting because of the high payout. Unfortunately, 30 for 1 is the equivalent of 29 to 1, nowhere near the 35 to 1 it should be, making these bets the worst in the game. This is an honor also shared with several other bets, including their neighbors, 1-2 and 5-6. Even if the payout is higher than 15 for 1 (14 to 1), these should be avoided.

You may hear someone call out a "horn" bet. It doesn't mean one chip is placed in the horn area (as seen on page 100). It's basically the same as a C & E bet, except that it's made in multiples of $4 and the chips are split between the 1-1, 1-2, 5-6, and 6-6 boxes, which we already mentioned are bad bets. Another bet that's fun to call out, but not good to risk your money on.

That leaves the "hardway" bets (as seen on pages 100 and 101). These are special bets that the point will be made with doubles. In other words, a player betting the "hard eight" wants a 4-4 to appear before either a 2-6, 3-5, 5-3, 6-2, or any 7. This seems pretty particular. Unfortunately, all the hardways are particularly bad bets with house advantages around 10%.

All of these prop bets are bad. They shouldn't be made separately or in an attempt to "hedge" each other or your pass line bets. When you add a bad bet to a good one, it doesn't strengthen the bad one, it weakens the good one. In other words, the best you can do is a pass, come, don't pass, or don't come with full maximum odds. Anything else you do weakens your play.

We've seen a variety of craps bets, ranging in house advantage from under 1% to over 16%. These bets represent a lot of potential activity at a busy table. Chips, jargon, and emotions flying in

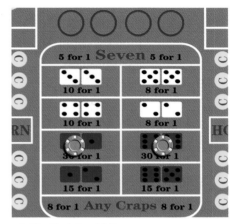

Betting the 1-1 and 6-6

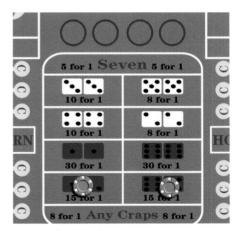

Betting the 1-2 and 5-6

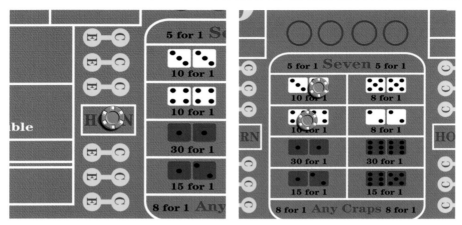

Horn bet

Hardway six and eight bets

every direction. So here are a few tips to help you enjoy the game:

- Rest any drinks or cigarettes under the rail, not on it.

- Stay focused on what you're doing.

- As soon as the stickman sends the dice to the shooter, the shooter is expected to roll them. So be on the lookout if you're making any last-second bets. If you interfere with the dice, you'll have a lot of unhappy people glaring at you!

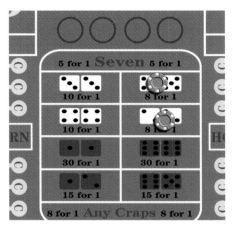

Hardway ten and four bets

• Remember to tip these hardworking dealers every so often, either with a straight chip or by placing the bet of their choice for them.

• Craps players are very superstitious, so you may want to avoid using the word "seven" more than you have to.

• Don't play "crapless craps." It's based on a gimmick that doesn't favor players.

• If a few point numbers start hitting (the start of a "monster" roll), consider risking 50% more on pass (or similar) bets. As it is literally a "crapshoot," that's the only way to come out ahead in the long run.

> "We must believe in luck. For how else can we explain the success of those we don't like?"
>
> —*Jean Cocteau (1889–1963), French writer*

Baccarat—with a silent "t"—has quite an extensive pedigree, having traveled from fifteenth-century Italy to the French Riviera, and then to South America and Cuba before being introduced to Las Vegas in the late 1950s. Along the way, it built a classy reputation as being the game of choice for high society. To this day, it retains that somewhat-snooty status, often being played in a separate high-roller area. In fact, it may be the only game whose mere name conjures up a dress code! But while *punto banco*, as it is also known, may sound fancy, it's actually the easiest table game to play.

Full baccarat layout

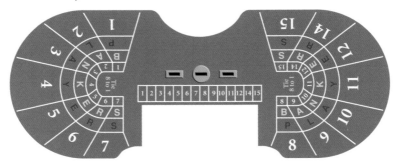

Aces are worth one.

Typically, as many as twelve to fourteen players can gather around a full baccarat layout. All of the numbers simply refer to each player's position around the table. Every player bets on whether the punto (player) or banco (bank) will have a better hand. Unlike with blackjack, you don't have to think about whether you want another card. The two hands play themselves out according to specific rules for drawing (as discussed later).

Face cards and 10s are worth zero.

The goal is for each hand to get as close as possible to a total of nine. Aces are worth one and face cards and 10s are worth zero. Every other card is worth its face value. Suits don't matter and it is impossible to bust in this game because double-digit numbers only count as

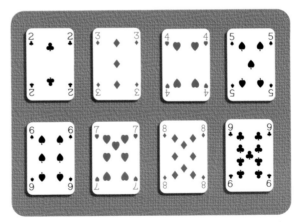

All other cards are worth their face value.

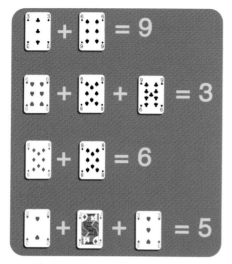

Double-digit numbers only use the second digit.

their second digit. Thus, for example, a 23 is just a 3 and a 16 is just a 6. For those familiar with blackjack, it can take a little while to get used to totaling the cards this way.

To start each hand, each bettor places a wager on either the punto or the banco in their particular area of the table. (You may notice the numbers 4 and 14 missing from the layout due to Asian superstition and/or the number 13 missing due to Western superstition.) A casino dealer may play the part of

A wager on banco

A wager on punto

banco, but sometimes the "sabot" (card shoe) is passed around so that each player actually gets a chance to deal (sort of like how the dice are passed in craps). Either way, the person dealing alternates dealing cards to the punto and banco hands so that each winds up with two. The banco hand is tucked under the shoe for the moment. The punto hand is delivered (either by sliding the cards across the felt or, in Europe, via a large paddle) to the player who wagered the most on the punto, giving that player the first peek at the hand, and then the cards are sent back to the dealer. The dealer then turns over both hands.

If either hand is a "natural," totaling eight or nine, play stops and whichever hand has a higher total wins. Otherwise, the punto acts first and the banco follows with a play based on what will avoid losing a majority of the time.

With a total of six or seven, the punto must stand. Logically, that signals the banco to draw with a total of zero through five or stand with a total of six or seven.

With less than six, punto must draw. If banco totals between zero and two, banco must draw. For the rest of the situations in which punto draws, banco draws depending on banco's total and what card punto draws (not punto's total).

A "natural" eight or nine

Punto must stand.

Banker has:

Player stands

Banker would stand.

Various ways to get less than six

Banker has:

Player draws:

Banker would draw.

If banco has three and punto draws an eight, banco stands. Otherwise, banco draws.

If banco has four and punto draws an eight up through ace, banco stands. Otherwise, banco draws.

If banco has five and punto draws a four through seven, banco draws. Otherwise, banco stands.

With six, banco only draws if punto draws a six or seven. And no matter what punto draws, Banco always stands with seven.

Again, these rules leave no room for choices (other than the size of your bet), which means you don't need to memorize them or plan a strategy. The two hands will either wind up with two or three cards. A win on

Banker would draw.   *Banker would stand.*   *Banker would stand.*

HOW BANCO ACTS

STANDS WITH:	WHEN:
A natural (nine or eight)*	Always
Seven	Always
Six	Punto stands
*By either Punto or Banco	

DRAWS A THIRD CARD WITH:	WHEN PUNTO:
Zero through two	Doesn't have a natural
Three	Draws anything but an eight
Four	Draws a two through seven
Five	Draws a four through seven
Six	Draws a six or seven

Banker would stand.

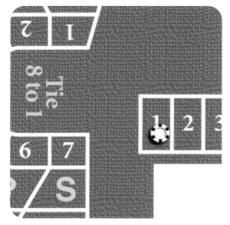

A token in the commission box

The tie

punto pays out even (1 to 1). A win on banco also pays out even minus a 5% commission to balance out the fact that banco wins more often based on the drawing guidelines. You don't pay the commission immediately. A token is placed in the middle of the table in your designated commission box and you settle up all your tokens before you leave the table.

The house advantage for betting on punto is 1.36% and on banco it is 1.17% (factoring in the commission). This makes either bet very good in comparison to most of the other games in the casino and is a good reason why high rollers don't mind wagering large sums of money in baccarat. The game does offer one other bet, the tie, a wager that punto and banco will "push" or "standoff" the next hand. Its relatively weak payout gives the tie bet around a 14% house advantage, giving you a good reason never to make that wager.

Baccarat Facts:

• In baccarat's French counterpart, chemin de fer, the player acting as banco (wagering the most money) must cover all losing bets on banco, but gets to collect all its winning bets, minus a 5% casino "rake" (commission). Also, there is some flexibility and decision making involved with either hand, drawing a third card on certain totals.

• Mini-baccarat is played at what looks like a blackjack table in the main pit area with smaller stakes but with the same good odds.

• Barona Valley Ranch Resort and Casino in Southern California offers cash baccarat (rather than using chips).

• When players are the dealers, they do have an option, but it's expected that they bet banco.

• Don't bother tracking the history of the hands' outcome on paper or by looking at the toteboard. It doesn't help. (If it did, do you think the casino would allow you to do it?)

> "Luck never gives, it only lends."
> —*Swedish proverb*

SIC BO

This ancient Chinese game is known throughout Asia as *tai sai* (big-small), *cu sic* (guessing dice), and in the Philippines as "hi-lo." It is relatively new to the United States. Although *sic bo* translates to "dice pairs," it actually uses three dice. The object of the game is to guess the individual numbers or combination of numbers that will appear on the dice after they are shaken in a tumbler.

Sic bo table layout

As you can see from the complex table layout, sic bo offers dozens of bets whose payouts range from 1 to 1 all the way up to as high as 180 to 1. However, only two of those bets are even remotely worth wagering money on. Naturally, they're the ones with the lowest payouts.

Bets on "small" (totals between 4 and 10) or "big" (totals between 11 and 17) yield a fair 2.78% house advantage, based on the fact that they don't pay on triples. In other words, a roll of 1-6-2 would pay out 1 to 1 for those who wagered small. But despite the fact that it totals between 11 and 17, a roll of 5-5-5 would not result in a payout for any players who wagered on big.

Although the payouts for many of the other bets vary from casino to casino, the house advantages generally range from a poor 9% to a preposterous 30%. Those are definitely the ones to avoid! But just so you know what they mean, here's a breakdown:

Each of the six single-number bets along the bottom of the table is a wager that a particular number will show on the three dice. It pays 1 to 1, 2 to 1, or 3 to 1, based on whether your number occurs once, twice, or three times among the three dice. So if you wagered on four, a 4-1-4 roll would pay 2 to 1.

Likewise, just above the single-number bets, a bet on one of the two-number bets is a wager that a particular non-double combination will occur. It's only possible to win one time per bet. So with that same 4-1-4 roll, a wager on 1-4 would get paid once at 5 to 1. Hopefully, the 16.67% house advantage would dissuade you from placing such a bet.

Just above the middle are the bets that the three dice will total anything from 4 through 17—easy enough to understand, but most of them range between 10% and 20% house advantages—a few of them are even worse! These bets are ten times worse than anything you'd even want to consider wasting your money on.

To the right of the small and left of the big, you can bet that a particular double (also known as "two of a kind") will occur. These are even worse than the regular two-number bets.

Betting on a particular triple, or "three of a kind," offers the highest payout, usually 150 or 180 to 1. But since the actual odds are 215 to 1, it gives a gigantic advantage to the house.

You might think a bet on "any triple" (top center) would be better, but the payout is scaled down from the individual triple payouts and is therefore just as bad.

Why do people bother playing a game with such horrific odds? Maybe some are attracted to the rattling dice or the big table layout. Or the fact that it lights up particular betting areas based on what wins. But bells and whistles aside, this game isn't a good choice for the player whose goal is to keep money in the wallet.

You may have seen another three-dice game in the casinos called chuck-a-luck. It offers a similar, but simpler, gaming experience. Comparable to the big and small wagers in sic bo, chuck-a-luck offers "high" (over 10) and "low" (under 11) as well as "odd" and "even." As with big and small, each of these bets pays even and doesn't win on triples, giving the house a 2.78% advantage on each. The single-number bets are similar, but tend to offer higher payouts if a triple shows. For instance, if you bet on two, you might get 10 or 12 to 1 on a 2-2-2—better, but a far cry from what you should get paid! And lastly, chuck-a-luck also offers a "field" bet that the dice will total 5, 6, 7, 8, 13, 14, 15, or 16. Similar to craps, it may look good, but it's not worth it in the long run.

"What is luck? It is not only chance, it is also creating the opportunity, recognizing it when it is there, and taking it when it comes."

—*Natasha Josefowitz (1916–), U.S. scriptwriter*

PAI GOW TILES

Although *pai gow* translates to "making nines," this time-honored Chinese tile game is nowhere near as easy to learn as baccarat (where the best total is nine). Pai gow uses a deck (or set) of thirty-two domino-like tiles, each of which is black on one side and has between two and twelve spots on the other side. The particular pattern of spots matters, but it doesn't matter whether the spots are white or red. Within the deck, eleven of the tiles repeat and ten are unique. This creates sixteen "pairs," using eleven actual doubles plus five assigned doubles.

Gee joon

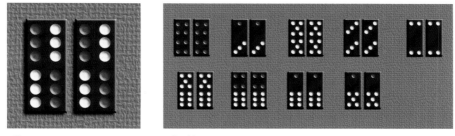

Teen   Doubles

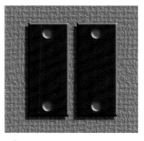

Day

The highest ranking pair is *gee joon* (supreme)—see below left. Next comes *teen* (heaven), shown above. And then *day* (earth), shown on the right.

Next in rank are the other nine doubles, as seen in the diagram above right. Starting in the upper left and going right, they are: *yun* (man), *gor* (goose), *mooy* (flower), *chong* (long), *bon* (board), *foo* (hatchet), *ping* (partition), *tit* (long leg seven), and *look* (big head six).

These are followed by the aptly named mixed pairs, as seen in the diagram below: *chop gow* (mixed nine), *chop bot* (mixed eight), *chop chit* (mixed seven), and *chop ng* (mixed five).

Chop gow, chop bot, chop chit, and chop ng

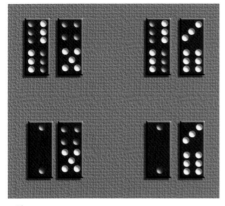

The wongs

Next comes a special category, the *wongs*, which are shown at left. Those in the top row, with double sixes and nines, are "kings of heaven." Those of the bottom row, with double ones and nines, are "kings of earth."

The wongs are followed by another special category, the *gongs*, which are shown below. In the gongs, each of the double sixes and eights is called a "treasure of heaven." Each of the figures with the double ones and eights is called a "treasure of earth."

The gongs, part one

The gongs, part two

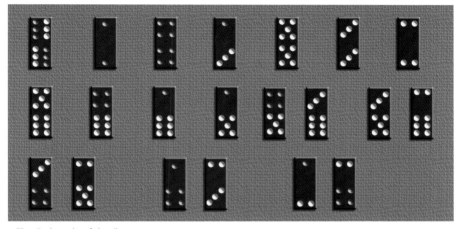

The single ranks of the tiles

The single ranks of the tiles are shown above. What's interesting to note is that the last two (the "wilds," seen on the right) individually rank the lowest and have different numbers of spots, but form the highest pair by adding to nine. Speaking of which, any other two tiles that aren't a pair, wong, or gong are ranked by adding the number of spots and then using only the single digit (another similarity to baccarat). For example, a 6/6 added to any 7 (totaling nineteen spots) would be considered a nine. In fact, that particular combination or a 1/1 and any 7 is a strong set known as a "high nine." Zero is the lowest possible total for two tiles.

The wilds

Now that you know all the rankings, you're ready to play. After between two and eight players place their bets, three dice are rolled to determine who will be dealt the first of the four-tile hands, or stacks. Each player splits his hand into two sets of two tiles, which are automatically ranked as a high and a low hand. You win even money (1 to 1) if your high and low hands beat the banker's high and low hands. You lose if both your hands lose to the banker. And you "push" (tie) if one wins and one loses against the banker.

If your high or low hand matches the banker's high or low hand, that's called a "copy." Unfortunately, you lose any copies to the banker. Thus, if your two hands win and copy, it's an overall push; if they lose and copy, it's an overall loss. However, if two hands are not identical but have the same total, the higher-ranking tiles in each hand are compared. For instance, if you had a 6/6-1/4 and the banker had a 4/4-3/6, those are both sevens, but you'd win because your 6/6, as the highest-ranking tile, beats a 4/4. If the totals and high tiles both match, it's a tie, which goes to the banker.

You probably noticed that in talking about the hands, we've referred to you and the "banker" instead of you and the "dealer." That's because another feature that pai gow has in common with baccarat is that each player gets a chance to be the banker, must cover the other players' bets, and pays a 5% on all net winnings. A player who utilizes a good strategy for splitting the hands and maximizes their bets as banker can have a low combined house advantage hovering around 1.5%.

Quirky Facts about Pai Gow Tiles

• Each four-tile hand can be split three possible ways.

• If two hands both total zero, the higher-ranking tiles are not compared and that hand is considered a push.

• As individual tiles, either gee joon (again, the 1/2 or 2/4) can be counted as a three or six and is never used to break a tie between hands with the same total.

• A third of the time, it's possible to split the tiles simultaneously into the highest possible high and highest possible low hands (which you should do, keeping in mind the above pairs and singles rankings).

> "It is a great piece of skill to know how to guide your luck even while waiting for it."
>
> —*Baltasar Gracian (1601–1658), Spanish writer*

Adding the American poker context to the traditional Chinese pai gow format makes for an interesting merger. Variations of pai gow poker have been played for a while, but only became popular as recently as the mid-1980s in California card houses. The game's flexible strategy, modest pace, and relative simplicity helped it spread to Las Vegas, Atlantic City, and beyond.

Pai gow poker shouldn't be confused with Chinese poker or full deck poker.

Pai gow poker is played at a blackjack-like table with a fifty-three-card deck. That includes a semiwild "bug" (joker), which can be used as an ace or to fill a straight, flush, or straight-flush. After players place their bets, a random number is generated, either with three dice or electronically, in order to determine which player is dealt the first hand (for reference, the dealer corresponds to the numbers one, eight, and fifteen). After each position, including the dealer, receives seven cards, players pick them up, separate them into hands of five and two, and place them down on the table.

The five-card hands are sometimes referred to as the "back" or "bottom" hands and the two-card hands as the "front" or "top" hands. This is a reflection of their typical placement on the table layout. When referring to their relative values, the five-card is "high" and the two-card is "low"—which can lead to all sorts of confusion when referencing the hands' positions and values!

The dealer then turns over her cards and separates them into hands of five and two according to the "house way" (specific guidelines that vary slightly from casino to casino). Each player's hands are then compared to the dealer's. If both of the player's hands beat the dealer's corresponding hands, the player's cards and wager are left on the table. If the player wins one hand but loses the other, the dealer taps the table to indicate a "push" (an overall tie, which occurs about 40% of the time) and takes the cards but leaves the wager. If both the player's hands lose to the dealer's, the dealer takes both that player's cards and wager.

In the event of a "copy" (an exact match of rank, usually on the two-card hands), the player loses that particular hand. So if the player wins the big hand and copies the little one, it's a push overall.

The dealer then pays off each winning wager around the table at even money (1 to 1) minus a 5% commission.

> As a courtesy, if you have the proper commission (25 cents on a $5 bet, 50 cents on $10, $1 on $20, etc.), put it next to your original wager in order to make the process of paying out the bets run smoother. (If you don't have the right denomination for the commission, the dealer can make change.)

The five-card hands are ranked as in poker, except that a "wheel" (ace-2-3-4-5) is considered the second-highest straight. (For a poker refresher, see the next chapter.) The two-card hands are either a pair (aces are best) or just high card (2-3 would be the worst). The most important rule in setting your hands is to make sure your five-card hand beats your two-card hand. In other words, if your two-card hand had an ace-king (which is very good), your five-card hand would need at least a pair. And if your two-card hand had a pair, your five-card hand would need a better pair. This is to prevent players from stacking their two-card hands to force a tie. If you don't set your hands properly, it's a "foul" and you automatically lose both hands.

The easiest hand to set is a "pai gow," a hand that doesn't contain any pairs or better. As with the hand on the right, the logical strategy is to keep the highest card in the high hand and to form the low hand with the second- and third-highest cards. The worst possible hand would be an eight-high pai gow (8-7-6-4-3-2-A with no five of the same suit).

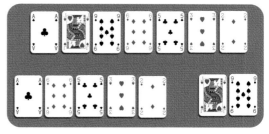

With no pairs, keep the highest card in the high hand.

A pair is also usually quite easy to play—especially with an ace in the low hand. The goal is to make the low hand as high as possible by at least getting an ace in there.

With one pair, make the low hand as high as possible.

With no ace, split underpairs (sevens or lower, as seen in the hand on the right) by putting the lower pair in the front hand. With an ace to make the front hand strong, keep two pair together.

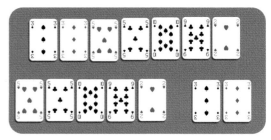

With two pairs, put the lower pair in the front hand.

With an ace in front hand, keep pairs together.

Split overpairs with other weak cards.

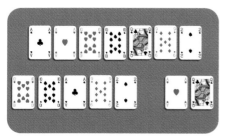

With two overpairs, put an ace in front hand.

Split aces if it is your only pair.

Split two overpairs (sevens or higher) with weak cards. And again, if with two overpairs it is possible to put an ace in the front hand, do so—even if that means splitting a pair of aces.

Likewise, you'd want to strip an ace from a pair of aces if it were your only pair and also from three aces with weak cards, with the hope of at least winning with the front hand for a tie overall.

The flush hand is virtually a guaranteed push overall

Split three aces to strengthen the front hand.

Flush hands can produce weak front hands.

because of the weak front hand. But the only logical alternate hand (with king-10 in front) would be likely to lose on both counts.

If your entire hand is the same suit, put the highest two cards in your front hand. You'll have a flush in the back hand either way, so you might as well form your best possible two-card hand!

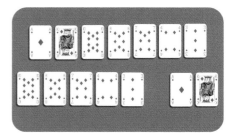

If all cards are suited, put the highest two in front.

Likewise, if there are more than five cards to a straight, then put the lowest possible straight into the five-card hand.

If you have to choose between a straight and flush, do whichever makes your front hand stronger. Similarly, you might not even want to keep a straight

More than five cards to a straight

With a straight or flush, make the best front hand.

Ignore the straight and split the pairs.

Using the joker as an ace

with a hand like the one in the middle picture on the left. Instead of expecting a tie, you might be able to pull off a win by splitting those nines and sevens.

The picture at the bottom left is a clear example of when to use the bug (joker) as an ace. But especially when you get a bug, it's important to also check for how it could be used to fill a straight or flush.

Three pair is another fun, easy hand to play. Since you're always looking to strengthen your front hand, put the highest pair up top and then keep the other two on the bottom hand. A similar sort of play occurs when a hand contains any threes of a kind. A three of a kind in the back hand is always good, so strip a pair from the higher three of a kind and put it in front.

Although it may be tempting to attempt to crush the dealer's high hand by keeping a full house together, it can prove to be overkill and therefore it's better to split it up.

Using a joker in a straight

Using a joker in a flush

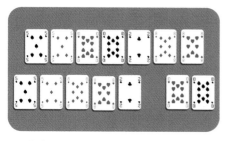

With three pair, put the highest pair in front.

Keep the lower three of a kind in back.

Four of a kind is a little trickier. With a low one (sevens or less), try to keep them all together and go for the almost guaranteed tie. But with a high one, go ahead and split them into pairs. If, instead of a king-5 alternate front hand, you'd had an ace-10 or better, you might have thought about keeping the monster quad queens together.

Always split a full house.

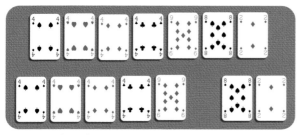

With a low four of a kind, keep them together.

With a high four of a kind, split them into pairs.

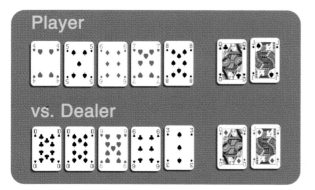

A frustrating tie

The hand on the bottom left is an example of a frustrating tie (since the queen-jack copy goes in favor of the dealer). The hand at the top on the opposite page is a tie as well, with a breath-holding near copy in back and pulse-raising tight win up front. Along similar lines, the hand at the bottom on the opposite page is a heartbreaking loss. So close, you'll stare at the cards in an attempt to somehow change them through the power of telekinesis!

The hand at the top of page 130 shows a tie. You win with the two pair but lose with the ace-jack. If you'd split the two pair, you'd still have tied, since the queens would have lost to the dealer's kings but the threes would have beat the dealer's twos.

And lastly, one of the other interesting phenomena of pai gow is the ability not to lose with a wretched hand. Your queen-high pai gow, as seen on page 130, is demolished in the back by the dealer's flush, but just wins up front, giving way to a life-saving tie.

In the end, it's nice to be able to hold the cards and make decisions. And with all the ties, your money lasts a while in this game. Depending on both your strategy and

A tie with near copy in the back

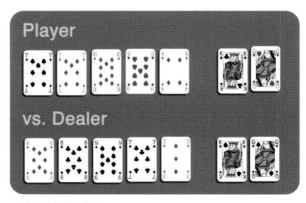

A heartbreaking loss

A tie—you win with the two pair but lose with ace-jack.

A life-saving tie

the "house way," the house edge is typically between 2% and 3%. But just as with regular pai gow (with tiles), you have the chance to play banker. Before the cards are dealt, the dealer puts a small tile (which often says "banker 2") in front of the player whose option it is. (The option rotates every hand.) If you can cover everyone else's bets and wish to be banker, you should, since by maximizing your banker bets (and playing smart overall strategy), you can lower the overall house advantage to under 2%. If you refuse the right to be banker, you can still have fun as a player.

Alternative Versions of Pai Gow Poker:

• "No push" is a gimmick that produces around a 4% house edge.

• Some California casinos offer a "completely wild" joker— and they don't mean that drunk guy sitting next to you. Seriously though, a bug that can turn into any card to help the player's hand is a good thing.

• "Jackpot" allows a $1 side bet that progressively pays off a variable amount (as shown on an ever-changing electronic tote board) for hands of four of a kind or better. Generally a waste of money.

• "Fortune" lets players make a $5 side bet that pays not only a fixed bonus payout on hands of three of a kind and higher, but also an "envy bonus" if any player gets four of a kind or better. The house edge on this one is inversely proportional to the number of players. In other words, it's probably not worth it unless at least four other people are playing (regardless of whether they make the side bet).

POKER

Long gone are the days when poker was played only by ruthless outlaws in saloons and shifty riverboat gamblers or completely dominated by roving professional hustlers like Doyle Brunson and Amarillo Slim. Nowadays, men and women of every age, locality, walk of life, and skill level are playing poker in its various forms.

Technology is playing a big part in the game's recent popularity. Television has enabled millions of viewers to see not only what cards the big tournament players are holding, but also their calculated chances of winning. Thus we have a context for all the bets and bluffs the pros make. The Internet has allowed millions to not only practice on their own for free, but play online tournaments with real money to win seats at live tournaments, which have grown exponentially in the last few years.

So when you walk into a casino or card house, you can expect to find more people playing more varieties of poker more frequently than ever. Of those varieties, without a doubt, Texas hold 'em is the current favorite, followed by seven-card stud and Omaha hold 'em. Each game is a very different animal. But as poker games, they all share at least seven major qualities:

1. You're playing directly against other players. Unlike most other casino games, you're not struggling against the house. Thus, although the game does have an element of chance in how the cards are dealt, skill is the overriding factor in poker. Luck may help or hurt in the short run, but in the long run stronger players who understand the game's intricacies will win and weaker players who ignore them will lose. In the meantime, the casino makes its money either by taking a "rake" (a certain percentage of each hand) or charging a "drop" (a time-based player fee).

2. Etiquette is essential. Despite the fact that you're competing against others for money, it's still important to maintain good sportsmanship. This means generally being amiable and not doing anything that could give you or another player an advantage over the rest. You should never discuss your or anyone else's hand while it is being played. In fact, you shouldn't even allude to what you had when you're not in the hand anymore. That information could help a player still in the pot! If by accident a player happens to see part of your hand, show everyone else as well. Other than that, act properly in turn (not betting until the person before you has); always keep your cards guarded, but in sight of the other players (so no cheating can be inferred); and be sure to treat the dealers with respect (especially by tipping, or "toking," them when you win).

3. Position is powerful. Where players are seated around the table in relation to the action is especially important as the number of players increases. In hold 'em games, the higher number of players you might face has strong implications for how likely various hands are to appear. And therefore, for how you should play whatever hand you're dealt, given where you sit. You might bet completely differently with the same cards in an early position (sooner to act) versus a later position.

4. Betting is crucial. The number of rounds of betting—especially in relation to what cards are seen at those betting intervals—defines the game dynamic. How you bet certainly matters. If you're first to bet or no one else has bet anything, you can either "check" (pass) or bet. Once a bet has been made, subsequent players can "call" (match the bet), "raise" (increase the bet), or "fold" (voluntarily forfeit the hand). This sets up an interesting strategic play: the "check-raise." Rather than make a huge bet, you could check first (appearing weak), wait for another player to bet (at whatever level they're comfortable), and then raise them (appearing strong). Ultimately then, a game's structure is tempered by its "limits"—how much a player can bet at any one time:

- In "fixed-limit" seven-card stud and hold 'em, the preset maximum you can bet or raise for the first two rounds is usually doubled from the third round on. So you'll typically hear about a "$3/$6 game" or "$10/$20 game." Although sometimes the limits are specified for each round, as in a "$10/$15/ $15/$20 game."

- A "spread-limit" game defines a range of acceptable minimum and maximum bets. Raises are often required to be at least as much as the previous bet. Thus, in a "$2 to $10" game, after a bet of $3, you couldn't bet $5 ($3 with a $2 raise). You'd have to bet at least $6.

- With "pot limit," you can bet as much as is in the pot. This includes your current bet. So if $50 were in the pot, you could bet up to $150—a simultaneous $50 call (for what was in the pot) and $100 raise (for what would be in the pot after your $50).

• "No limit" means that you can bet up to however many chips you have in front of you. If any bet puts you "all in" (leaving you with no more chips), you lay no claim to any further bets for the rest of that hand. Those bets would be put into a side pot against multiple players. (There'd be no point in just one other player continuing to bet against you when all your money's already in the pot.) Thus, you can't win or lose more chips than you have.

The three types of limit games (as opposed to no limit) are often further qualified as "low-limit" ($2/$4, $3/$6, and $5/$10), "medium-limit" ($10/$20, $20/$40, and $30/$60), and "high-limit" ($50/$100 and higher). In any of the limit games, typically the number of "bumps" (raises) in any round of betting is capped at three or four, depending on the particular rules of the game in that casino. Speaking of which, when you do raise, it's good to verbally declare your intention. (Nothing fancy, as long as the word "raise" is in there.) Or you can just put the chips for a raise in without saying anything. What you want to avoid is a "string bet," saying that you call or putting in the chips for a mere call and then saying that you raise. Turning what should be one fluid motion into two is unfair here for the same reason that a balk in baseball is unfair—it throws off the timing of the next player.

5. Reading is fundamental. After all, poker isn't just about cards. It's about an interpersonal psychological battle. Therefore, you need to glean whatever information you can from your opponents. You do this by "reading" them, paying attention to how they act and react in certain situations. For instance, a particular player might make a big bet, avoid eye contact with anyone, get called, and turn out to be bluffing. It's no guarantee, but the next time he or she makes a big bet and avoids eye contact, you'll have a strong clue about a potential bluff. That's why a key component of the game is playing the other players as much as you play the cards. In fact, to some degree, the cards don't matter much. A great player can watch how others react to their cards, bet, sit, stack their chips, fidget, talk, even breathe—or forget to, when they're nervous!—and take away information. Especially when you've folded and aren't in the hand anymore, pay attention to what the other players do. The flip side of the coin is that you also need to be aware of how you act. You need to consciously act differently. If you always play the same way, you might as well play with your cards facing outward.

A royal (straight) flush

Four of a kind, or "quads"

Full house

6. Better players think ahead. By keeping track of which cards are "dead" (already folded or in other players' hands), you can have a feel for how many "live" cards could help your hand. Based on the chances of getting those live cards, you can roughly figure the odds of getting your best possible hand. But when you bet, you also need to consider other players' best possible hands as well. On the way to your potential straight, you don't want to bet a minimum that makes it easy for another player to wait for a flush!

It works the other way too. If you have a powerful hand that could win without improving (like an already-made full house), then you might want to allow the other players to bet without raising them until the last two rounds, when they're already psychologically committed to the hand. Thus, you always need to think about what bets have been made, what yours indicate about your cards, and what other players' bets tell about theirs—and therefore what the bet coming up should be.

To win at poker you either have to have the best hand or bet in a way that leaves you as the only remaining player in the hand.

Regular flush

Straight

Three of a kind, or "trips"

Two pair

Pair

7. The hands are figured similarly. The cards rank ace (occasionally low, usually high, and sometimes both), 2 through 10 (the numbered cards) and jack, queen, king (the "face" or "court" cards). The top hand is a straight flush—five cards of the same suit in sequential order— the very best of which is an ace-high "royal." After that, "quads" (four of a kind) is very powerful, followed by a "full house" or "full boat"—three of a kind and a pair in the same five cards. They're declared based on the three of a kind, thus the one on page 138 is "nines full of fours." Next is a regular flush—any five cards of the

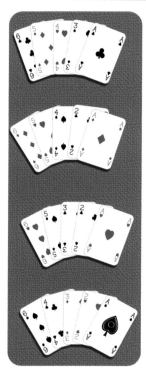

The second-best low

The best low and second-best straight

Six lows

same suit. Since flushes are measured by the highest card, the one on page 139 is a "king-high flush."

Next is a straight—any five nonsuited sequential cards. Straights are also measured by the high card, so the one on page 139 is a "nine-high straight." After straights come "trips" (three of a kind), then two pair, which is self-explanatory. An ordinary pair is shown on page 139—these 10s happen to have an ace "kicker," an unmatched card that would be more helpful if it paired up. And lastly, the lowest-ranked hands have all unmatched cards of different suits completely out of sequence, known as "nothing," "schmaltz," or "garbage." However, these hands can also be valuable.

In contrast to "regular" poker, in which the object is to get the highest hand possible, the goal of some poker games is to get the lowest hand possible—or in "split" games, either the highest or lowest hand. Since "lows" are nonpaired hands, they're measured by their highest cards. Thus, the best low in casinos is a five-high straight, also known as a "bicycle," "wheel," or "baby straight." After the only possible five-low come several possible six-lows (from best to worst): 6-4-3-2-A, 6-5-3-2-A, 6-5-4-2-A, 6-5-4-3-A, and 6-5-4-3-2.

Straight flush high and wheel low

You probably noticed that the wheel and this last one are technically straights. Whether a hand is a straight—or even a flush—doesn't factor into how "low" the hand is. In most casinos, it's just based on rank. So the ultimate would be a hand like the one on the right, since it's a straight flush high and a wheel low. This particularly powerful-but-rare hand is known as a "steel wheel."

When comparing lows, start with the highest cards first, then move on down the line. Whichever hand has the lower high cards is the better low. Usually it only takes a couple of cards to determine which low wins (such as a 6-4 beating a 6-5, or a 6-5-3 beating a 6-5-4). After the handful of six-lows, there are fifteen possible seven-lows and thirty-eight possible eight-lows.

Typically, eight is used as the "qualifier" to what lows are allowed. (That's what the "eight" on the end of "seven-card stud/ eight"—sometimes shortened to "seven-eight"—and "Omaha/eight" means.) In other words, if you don't have five cards all eight or lower, it's not usually going to be considered a low. Which, given the number of opponents who could have any of the fifty-six possible eight-or-better lows, makes sense.

Seven-Card Stud

At the start of any seven-card stud game, all the players "ante" by putting a relatively small amount into the pot. In a low-limit game such as $2/$4, the ante might be 50 cents. When the pot is right, the dealer deals every player who anted two "hole" cards (facedown) and an "up" card (faceup). Players are allowed to peek at their hole cards, but must leave them facedown on the table. The player with the lowest "door card" (first up card) "brings in" the hand by making the first bet, something between the ante and lower max bet. In this case, $1 would be appropriate.

The "door card" (also known as "Third Street").

If more than one player has the same low
door card, it goes by lowest suit (clubs,
diamonds, hearts, and then spades). This is
the only time in poker that suit is used as a
basis for ranking.

As after any bet, the next player to the left can call (bet
$1), raise (put in a total of $2 to "complete the bet" or
$3 to bump the max), or fold by "mucking" their cards
(turning them over and sending them toward the
dealer). The betting goes around until
every player has either folded or called
every bet and raise. Assuming more than
one player is still in the pot, a fourth
card—sometimes called "Fourth
Street"—is dealt. This time, the player
with the highest cards showing (usually
a pair or at least a face card) bets first.

Fourth Street

Again, assuming multiple players are still
in it, "Fifth Street" is dealt. This is a key
junction, not only because five cards
enable making a full hand, but also
because the limit doubles. In this
example, players can now bet or raise
up to $4 on any bet. Predictably, "Sixth
Street" comes next, also dealt up and
followed by a bet. "Seventh Street" is

Fifth Street

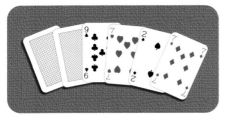

Sixth Street

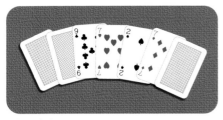

Seventh Street

Trip sevens

then dealt down, followed by a final bet and "showdown" (players reveal their cards to see who has the best hand). Thanks to a seven in the hole, our sample hand (as shown on the bottom left) wound up trip sevens. Not bad, but not likely to win against six or seven other players.

The image at the top of page 145 shows the start of a good low. In seven-eight, you might start betting aggressively right away to send a signal to your only apparent competition (the player with the seven). Whereas in "razz" (seven-card stud with just one winner low), you'd probably "slowplay" this hand, checking or betting the minimum for a couple of rounds. By playing the hand soft this way, you allow your weaker competition to contribute more to the pot. When the max doubles at Fifth Street and you're likely to have received a five, four, or ace to strengthen your hand even further—that will be a better time to bet the limit.

While the hand on the right in the middle has obvious high potential (as an "inside straight" draw), the only reason to have stayed in with it in razz would be if everyone checked both rounds. It's still not a great reason to be in the hand, but never fold if you can get a free ride! Another bad razz situation would develop with the hand on the bottom right. The ace and six were both good low "scare cards" (outwardly indicating strength). But it'd be tough to bet as if the 10 helped you and you realistically don't have a shot at anything low. Definitely one to abandon.

The hand on page 146 shows an interesting low situation. You'd extract the 7-4-3-2-A, also known as a "seven-four" or "smooth seven." It's the best possible seven-low, but as we saw above, beatable by several six- and five-lows. A better version of that hand would be the hand on the bottom left. In seven-eight, it presents not only an okay low but also a decent high (flush

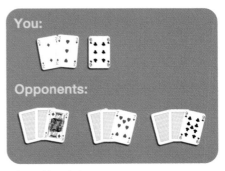

A good low start

Has high potential as an inside straight draw

Another bad razz situation

An interesting low hand

An okay low, with a decent high

in diamonds). In fact, with a hand like that, it'd be possible to win either half of the pot—or maybe even "scoop" (win the whole pot, both high and low). However, a more likely scooping hand is the one at the top on page 147.

Your seven-high straight's major competition is Player Two, with the possible full house or four jacks. If Player Two's been betting heavy the whole time, that's dangerous. But if she only started betting on Sixth Street, it points to just having trip jacks (which you can beat). On the low end, you have a nice 6-5. Player Three would need to be hiding an ace plus either a five or four to beat you in that direction. Again, base your decision on that player's betting history. Likewise, how you've been betting the hand will tell more than the ace-3-7-10 you have showing will. Given the steady progression of cards to your strong low, you should've been betting big the whole way. And since both your high and low are effectively hidden, you'll be a tricky read (which is good).

After folding, you sit back, watch the players (opposite) duke it out, and try to get a read on them.

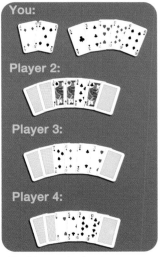

Player Two bets the max and therefore might have already made his straight. But Player One raises back into Player Two. What could Player One have? Three kings is his best possible hand. But that's not enough to beat the straight that Player Two is representing. One guess is that Player One has the 10-jack of hearts (or 10-queen or jack-queen) in the hole, for an inside straight flush draw. Or it could be a regular flush draw and a probe bet. If Player Two folds, you know both that he was bluffing and that he can be scared out of a pot. If he calls, it means he's either still drawing to the (incomplete) straight or trying to trap Player One. And if he raises back, he either has the straight or could be bluffing as well. Focus on what Player Two does here and you'll learn a lot!

Possible scooping hand

As you watch the three contenders go at it on Fourth Street (see page 148), Player Three is first to act with sixes and checks. Player One checks the possible flush. And Player Two bets the max. A call by Player Three would indicate weakness, allowing Player Two to dictate the tempo and stay in to possibly improve. Of course, it's possible that Player Two simply has another eight or nine in the hole, which would put him slightly in the lead. Player

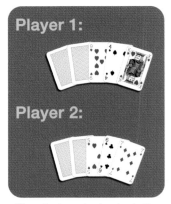

Player One's reraise signals what?

Player 1:

Player 2:

Player 3:

Three-way play at Fourth Street

Three will probably raise, "advertising" (indicating) a third six hidden and putting Player Two to the test. Again, how Player Two bets here will tell a great deal about him as a player (assuming he stays in to the end, giving you a chance to play back his every move in your head).

The difference between a good player and great player at seven-card stud is that a good player can figure all the reasons to stay in and a great one can figure the right reasons to get out. Any of the early hands in the picture below are good enough to play. But a hand like the starter shown below left—

Good seven-card stud starting hands

A bad opening hand

with no pair and virtually no chance for getting a straight or flush—is a prime example of when to quit after the door card.

Both the flush draw and queens with possible flush are average examples of when to stay in on Fourth Street. You'd also obviously stay in at this

A flush draw and queens with possible flush

stage with a hand such as in the picture at right in the middle. Although trips like this might be good enough to win, they don't leave a lot of "outs" (alternative ways to improve) and are certainly at the mercy of higher trips, a straight, or better. The two pair in the picture at the bottom also seems good, but very few cards (other than the two fours and two sevens left in the deck) can help the two "underpair" to improve. The picture on page 150 shows a hand with an open-ended straight draw and a flush possibility. If either hit,

A hand with trips

Two pair

they'd be likely to "hold up" (and win). But if not, the hand has no chance. Therefore, play any of these last few hands cautiously. Speaking of which, although the hand at below left might give an overly optimistic player a thought of catching a straight or seven-six low, neither has a fair chance of hitting or winning. Don't chase hands like this last one!

A hand with an open-ended straight draw and flush possibility

This is a hand to quit as soon as possible.

Once we hit Fifth Street, it's more about comparing what you've got to what's showing on the "board" (faceup in other players' hands). In the large picture opposite, Player Two not only has a better pair, but one of the 10s you need to improve—both signs to fold! The picture at the top right shows another vulnerable two pair. Fine as far as a two pair goes, but the likelihood of catching a 10 or 9— which you could easily figure based on all the other players' up cards—isn't very strong. If vulnerable, it'd be better to have a hand like the one in the center. A draw to the "nut" (best possible) flush makes it probably

You:

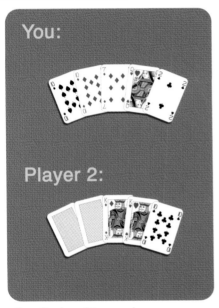

Player 2:

Player Two has a 10 you need.

Two pair, decent but vulnerable

This hand could be a possible nut flush.

You:

Player 2:

Two pair on Sixth Street

worth staying in here. But if you don't catch a spade, you'll have a serious mathematically based decision to make in the next round.

As the hand shown at right played out, you had thoughts of a high straight, but instead have two pair here on Sixth Street. Based on just the cards

This hand improved to a straight.

shown, you have a 1 in 10½ chance to beat Player Two's trip queens showing—assuming Player Two doesn't already have or improve to a full boat! The only reasons not to fold would be if Player Two makes a miniscule bet you could call for less than a tenth of what's in the pot (thus playing the "pot odds"), or if you believe Player Two is the type that could be bluffed out. But bluffing is tough to pull off in limit games, unless you're in a later position, facing a max of two opponents and have scare cards that indicate a very strong hand.

The hand above started off as a pair and actually improved to a straight. The only problem is that Player Two watched the hand develop and has been raising consistently since Fourth Street. It's possible that Player Two is going low (if the game permits) or bluffing (if he is the type to do so), but it is more likely that he hit a flush. Knowing he has you beat, he'll bet into you all day. This is where the different limits come into play. With fixed limit, it might actually make sense to call the last bet, just to keep Player Two honest. But with a sizable pot or no limit bet, you should quickly forget

about the money you already put into the pot and fold
on Seventh Street.

Texas Hold 'Em

Hold 'em players may put money in the pot before the
cards are dealt (in the form of "blinds," not antes), have
similar limits, and figure their best five of seven cards,
but the rest of this game is very different from stud. To
start, a "dealer" button is placed in front of one of the
players, who is said to be "on the button." The two
players just to the left of the button are responsible that
round for supplying forced bets (regardless of their
cards). The first player to the left of the button puts out
a "small blind"—$1, half the initial max in a $2/$4
game. And the next player to the left puts out the "big
blind"—$2, the initial max bet in the game. Every player
receives two cards. Since the first two players to the left
of the dealer have already posted bets, the player to
their left (three from the button) is the first to voluntarily
act. That player may call the $2 big blind, raise (in this
case, up to $2 more), or fold. When the action gets
back around, the small blind has to put in more money
or fold. The big blind is allowed to raise his own bet, or
if no one else raised, signal a call (requiring no more
money) by tapping the felt. The dealer then "burns" a

The flop

The turn is added.

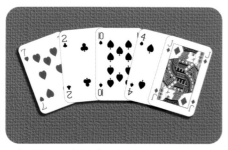

The river completes the common cards.

card (deals one off the top of the deck and out of play) and deals the "flop." These are three "common cards" that everyone can use in their hand, dealt faceup in the middle of the table. The betting from here on is normal, starting with the player to the left of the button (who posted the small blind), who may check or bet. After a round of betting, the dealer burns another card and deals the "turn" card faceup. Another round of betting ensues, with the limits now doubled. The dealer burns a third card and deals the "river" card face-up. A final round of betting takes place, and then there's a showdown.

> The five "community" (common) cards of the flop, turn, and river are collectively known as the "widow," "board," "table," or "field."

The first important thing to know is which initial hands are worth holding on to. Because as many as nine or ten players can be seated around the table,

what's playable is definitely a matter of position. In an early position (the first few seats after the dealer), you'll fold most of the time, but stay in with high pairs or high cards with straight or flush possibilities.

> Because they give both straight and flush opportunities, "suited connectors" (cards in sequence of the same suit) are valuable holdings.

Initial hands worth holding on to in an early position

In a middle position, it's okay to play medium pairs, aces and kings with slightly lesser cards, suited connectors, and high nonsequential straight draws. And late (toward or on the button), small pairs, aces and kings with little cards, low suited connectors, and any halfway decent straight draw are fair game. But those guidelines are general and can be tinkered with according to how aggressive or conservative you want to play.

Suited connectors

Good cards to play in a middle position

These are okay to play a late position.

The key after the flop is to realistically assess how and/or whether those three cards have helped your hand. For instance, the flop on the left on page 157 clearly has you in the lead at that point. So you'd obviously stay in, but how you'd bet is another story. Since many cards could make a straight or flush possible, you'd probably want to bet big to try to keep the dreamers out of the pot. The hand on page 157 in the center indicates a similar situation where you're in the lead for the moment with top pair, but think of how that would change if a club or nine showed on the turn. The tables are turned in the picture on page 157, upper right, where you're the one looking to fill an inside straight. If a 10 came on the turn, you'd make that straight, but a higher straight would be possible if a player held a king-jack.

Always look for ways you could be beat!

This flop has you in the lead.

You are leading with top pair.

An inside straight draw

As an exercise, compare the relative strength of the three straights flopped at right, in the center. The first is the weakest, since any player with a seven-jack or jack-queen would have a higher straight. The second gives you the "nuts" (best possible straight), but a six or seven on the turn or river could change that. The third is the best situation, because no single card could knock you off the top.

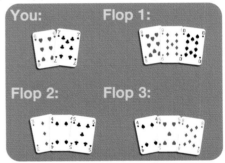

Three possible straights on the flop

The picture at the lower right shows a hand with potential, but if the turn doesn't pair your ace, help with your heart flush, or supply a king or jack to your straight, then it is wise think about folding. Even holdings that seem strong initially,

A hand with potential heartbreak!

Hooks (jacks)

It is worth seeing another card.

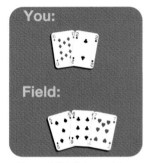

You could bluff the straight.

like the "hooks" (jacks) shown above on the left are vulnerable. With two higher cards on the board (the ace and queen), the chances are good that you're currently beat—but don't ditch the hand yet. Wait to see if the turn helps your straight. It's all about the possibilities!

The hand above in the center is nothing yet, but has over a dozen cards that could help the cause. In the picture above right, even though you know you've got a bad hand, in a late position against only a few players you could throw down a hefty wager—you'd be bluffing the straight. Players would either assume you had an eight-nine or peg you for faking. That's okay; part of bluffing is getting caught as players are more likely to call another big bet later on, when you have them beat!

Nut flush on the turn

Top flush

Top flush

For instance, in the hand above left, you caught the nut flush on the turn. No card on the river could possibly "counterfeit" your hand (make a better one possible). Bet big, especially if you've bluffed and been caught before! Compare that to the two hands on the right. In both cases you also have the top flush. The former should be slowplayed, so as not to be too obvious. Act hesitant and don't raise it up until at least the next round (when the limit is higher). In the other case, the seven fills your hearty flush, so you should lure in other players with an intermediate bet that makes it appear you're betting out of vulnerability after just having made a straight.

Always keep your opponents guessing.

A good semi-bluff hand

A vulnerable hand

Aces up

Betting large on the hand on the far left is what's known as a "semi-bluff." You don't have the best hand, but it is possible that you could improve your hand. Contrast that to the hand above on the right. You've already made a nice straight, but are vulnerable to a flush in spades, not to mention the unlikely, but potential, full house (for someone at this point with a pair of nines or sevens or a jack-nine or jack-seven). Even the best possible holdings, such as two aces, are vulnerable. As seen on the left, your Goliath starting hand could now be taken down by any player holding a lone two (giving them trip deuces that'd beat your two pair, "aces up").

Good Texas hold 'em is played like a chess game. You need to think both offensively and defensively with an end goal in mind. Are you the one setting the trap or about to be trapped? How many possible moves do you have? Thinking a few steps ahead, how do you want to play out this battle? What does your opponent's move tell you about what he's planning? What will you do if you're raised? These are but a few of the questions that fill each layer of this mathematical and psychological game. This is why the best players are quick to figure out both the odds and their opponents.

Strong hands

Omaha Hold 'Em

The blinds, betting, and community cards are the same as in Texas, but Omaha deals four cards instead of two. Plus, rather than using any combination of holdings and table cards, Omaha

Decent hands

Weak cards for Omaha

requires that you must use two from your hand and three from the widow. Omaha is often played high/low with an eight qualifier, whereas Texas is most often played with just one winner high. These three factors combine to form a strikingly different brand of hold 'em!

Strong hands (top) give several combinations of straights, flushes, and pairs, along with high cards. Decent hands (middle) have middle pairs and only a few straight and flush draws. The weakest initial cards (bottom) have lower, spread-out cards and lack face cards

Hand:

Widow:

Best:

This hand has just a two pair.

Hand:

Widow:

A full house

You:

Flop:

This hand misses full house.

The fact that each four-card holding yields six possible two-card combinations is powerful. It means that after the flop, you already have six possible hands, which, in turn, means that given the number of players, if a hand is possible, someone's likely to have it. So, if the board shows three to a straight or flush, assume that a player has the straight or flush (if not the best possible one). Likewise, if the board pairs up, assume someone out there has a full house. And since the board will pair up or show three to a straight or flush a large majority of the time, you need to not only be aware of your own best hand, but also what the overall best possible hand is (which both take practice figuring out).

For instance, the image at top left shows what seems like a great situation, but you don't have the boat (fives full of threes), just a lousy two pair. The image at above right shows another case of not getting a full house. To get a house, you need a situation like the one on the left, where your pair matches the board, or where two of your cards match a pair and single card

Hand:

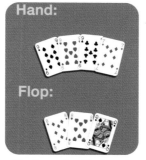

Flop:

Trips in your hand isn't good.

on the board (in this last example, a jack-five, queen-five, or two-five would've given you fives full). The bottom line is that having three of a kind in your starting hand isn't a good thing. Since you can only use two of them, it only lowers your chances at getting a great hand!

The way hands are figured also has implications on the low end. It means that the widow has to contain three cards of eight or less for there to be a low. If not, there's no possible way to form an eight-low or better. With no low, the game has just one winner high. This is why (as opposed to in Texas) having twos and threes in your hand in Omaha is valuable, such as in the hand on the top right. Likewise, even though the hand on the bottom right is weak high (the sixes aren't much help), it's worth staying in to see if another low card comes on the turn or river.

Aces with low cards are even better, since they give straight and flush prospects high as well as good low opportunities. The hand at the top left on page 164 is a good example of having both the nut flush and nut low

Hand:

Widow:

Low:

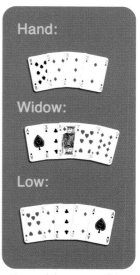

Twos and threes are useful.

You:

Flop:

This is a weak high hand.

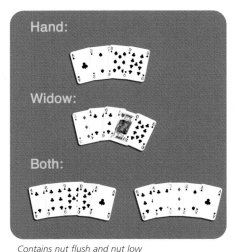

Hand:

Widow:

Both:

Contains nut flush and nut low

You:

Field:

This is not high or low.

You:

Flop:

A potential straight

using different cards within the same hand, thus giving you a strong shot at the whole pot. (Another player could also have a different ace-two, so you might have to split the low half of the pot, but that still gives you at least three-fourths of the pot!)

Even if you don't have a shot at winning low, you need to keep your eye on that half of the pot. For instance, in the picture at the top right, you're working on a potential straight. But with a low already possible on the flop, other players might drive up the price of poker to make you think twice about whether it's worth drawing to your possible straight.

More cards make for more possibilities, but you still need to fit the flop to your hand. At the very least, it shouldn't hurt you. In the picture at the bottom left,

An opened-ended straight

Tough hand to fold on turn

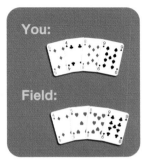

Four pairs with no straight

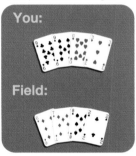

A potentially strong hand

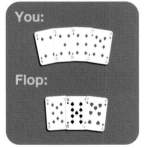

A straight on the flop

you should've folded after the flop because you're not high or low! The sevens and eights would've only been worth continuing after seeing a seven, eight, or strong straight opportunity in the flop. The hand at the top left did have an open-ended straight draw right on the flop. Though the widow teased with help toward a higher straight and another pair, all you wound up with were an unimpressive "set" of eights (three of a kind). The picture at above center led to more disappointment. The fully suited/connecting four-card holding seemed promising for a high straight or flush, but none of it panned out. Definitely a tough one to fold on the turn!

As we've seen above, matching cards isn't always a good thing. See top right for a case in point. The board's given you four pairs with no straight or flush draws! The only possible winner would be if another

You:

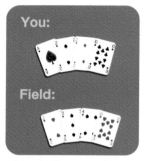

Field:

A hand with many options

You:

Flop:

Two possible full houses here

one of those cards showed up again on the table, but that's not likely.

At least the hand at the bottom right on page 165 has already hit a straight on the flop. Unfortunately, it's the weakest possible straight. Anyone with a six-ten or ten-jack has you beat. The hand at the center right on page 165 is the strongest one at the moment. But that could be short-lived. A nine, ten, or jack makes a higher straight possible and another diamond makes a flush likely!

> Always be thinking of what cards you'd most like (or not) to see next!

What card would you want to see on the river in the hand at the top left? A three, four, or ten would give you a full house. The "case" two (of clubs, the last one left) would give you four of a kind. Any spade would give you the nut flush. You could also make a straight. And any five, six, seven, or eight would give you the nut low. That makes the five of spades the ultimate river card for this hand. It would give you both a straight-flush high and the best possible low! In the absence of that dream card, you still have enough good ones that a big bet is warranted here on the turn.

Omaha is a game where you shouldn't bet the farm unless you have a hand that can't be "cracked" (beat even though it's strong). You actually have two different possible full houses in the hand at the bottom left on page 166, but, most importantly, by using the two kings you've got the best one possible (kings full of eights). The only way someone could beat your hand is by having four eights, which you know isn't possible, since you have one of the two eights they'd need!

A good hand can still lose, but you can win on bad losses in some casinos.

The weirdest part of it all is that getting beat isn't always a bad thing. Casinos sometimes offer a jackpot for "bad beats" based on losing with an otherwise great hand. The rules vary from casino to casino. To qualify, you usually have to have played a certain number of hands. Then, if you have a "pocket pair" (in the hole) or you at least tie the board and lose with a certain full house or better, you win part of a jackpot that builds with each pot. For example, take the hand on the right. The ace-queen wouldn't have qualified because of the king on the board. The ace-king tying the board would qualify you; but since you couldn't lose, you'd just win the hand high with no jackpot. You

would, however, qualify with the threes and could also potentially lose to anyone with a higher pair. If you did lose with the threes, you'd win a major part oi the jackpot, which would also get split among the winner of the hand and other big losers. It's nothing to try for, but could be a nice consolation prize for a huge hand that doesn't win.

Another interesting casino poker phenomenon is the "kill" factor. When playing with a kill, if any player wins two hands in a row, the limits automatically double until that player loses a hand. In other words, if you are in a $2/$4 game and win back-to-back hands, it becomes a $4/$8 game until you fold or get beat.

Once you feel you're ready to play for real in a casino, head to a poker room and tell the manager you'd like to play a low-limit game. (Based on interest from other players, you may have to wait for the manager to drum up a particular game.) Even if you're used to playing for bigger stakes on the kitchen table, it's a different game in the casino. The rules are different, the action is different, and the players are different. You won't be up against your buddies just looking to have a good time. Your competitors will probably have played more than you and be glad to take whatever money you put on the table! So be especially careful not to talk yourself into playing hands. Every bad decision you make (big or small) adds up over time. Ideal play is a blend of discipline and aggression. When you're done, log the action. That's right, keep a journal of how much you bought in with, if you bought any more chips during the game, and how much you left with. It's a good way to keep track of the dollars and your performance as a player.

"How can you say luck and chance are the same thing? Chance is the first step you take, luck is what comes afterwards."

—Amy Tan (1952–), U.S. novelist, from The Kitchen God's Wife

THREE-CARD POKER

PAIR PLUS

ANTE

PLAY

To play the main bet, place the bet in the ante area.

Bragg, an ancient precursor to poker played with three cards, has been played in Britain for centuries. It has an offshoot called "flush" that's played in India. And although bragg utilizes a different betting procedure, it's said to be the basis of all poker games. In 1994, Derek Webb, a successful professional poker player and proprietor of the British company Prime Table Games, adapted bragg for the casino, producing what we now

The lowest possible qualifying dealer hand

know as Three-Card Poker. Five years later, the Las Vegas–based company Shuffle Master bought the rights to the game. Part of the popularity of this relatively new game is in how easy it is to play.

You can place either of two independent wagers. The first is a straightforward wager that your hand will beat the dealer's. You place a bet (at least the table minimum) in the "ante" area. After seeing your hand, you can either fold or place a second bet (equal to the ante) in the "play" area. If the dealer's hand doesn't qualify with at least a queen-high (as seen above), you win the ante bet at 1 to 1 and keep your play bet.

If the dealer has at least a queen (which will happen about 70% of the time) and your hand beats the dealer's, you get paid 1 to 1 on both the ante and play bets. Of course, if the dealer's hand qualifies and beats yours, you lose both your ante and play bets. In the case

The minimum hand you should play with

of a tie, the hands push (neither wins and you keep both bets).

Computer simulations have shown the break-even hand you should play to be a queen-six-four. Playing that minimum means going ahead on any king- or ace-high hand (such as king-five-four or ace-four-two) or better. It wouldn't make sense to call with less than a queen-high, since you couldn't possibly win both of these bets. Calling with more makes sense, since you have a shot at beating a qualified dealer hand at least some of the time. And by refusing to forfeit the half dozen or so hands in between (queen-three-two to queen-six-three), you'll lose less in the long run.

Based on just that optimal queen-six-four strategy and the one payout, the house advantage is a belligerent 8.7%. To make it a more player-friendly game, a special bonus is paid out on the ante bet when your hand is a straight, three of a kind, or straight flush (as seen in the table on page 173). This brings the net house edge down to a somewhat more amiable 3.4%.

Hand	Ways to Make It	% of Hands	Ante Payout	Pair Plus Payout
Straight flush	48	0.22%	5 to 1	40 to 1
Three of a kind	52	0.24%	4 to 1	30 to 1
Straight	720	3.26%	1 to 1	6 to 1
Flush	1,096	4.96%	N/A	4 to 1
Pair	3,744	16.94%	N/A	1 to 1
Queen- to ace-high	9,720	43.98%	N/A	N/A
Jack-high or less	6,720	30.41%	N/A	N/A

The ante bonus is paid out regardless of the dealer's hand (qualifying or in relation to yours). So with the hands shown on the right, if you bet $5 on ante and another $5 on play, you'd lose the $10 in bets but get paid $20 on the bonus.

The game's second wager, the pair plus, is also made prior to the deal and is figured independently of the dealer's hand. You place a bet in the "pair plus" area and if your hand has at least a pair, you get paid according to the payout schedule shown in the table above. In other words, if you bet $5 on the pair plus and the hands came up as in the

This would get a $20 ante bonus.

Your Hand:

Dealer's Hand:

This would win $5 on a pair plus payout.

hand shown on the left, you'd win $5 even though your pair wasn't as good as the dealer's flush.

As you can see from the figures in the table, you'll lose the bet almost 75% of the time. But when you do win, it's at a rate that makes for a 2.3% house advantage. So if you really wanted to maximize your Three-Card Poker play, you could just bet pair plus and skip the main bet (with its 3.4% house advantage) altogether! Before you do that, however, make sure the particular table's payouts are as listed above. Some casinos will adjust the payouts in a way that may seem slight, but really hurts players. If, for instance, instead of 4 to 1 on flushes, a shifty casino were to pay only 3 to 1, just that little change more than triples the house advantage to over 7%! Bottom line: don't play the pair plus if the payouts are any less than the "full" 40-30-6-4-1.

A few last thoughts about Three-Card Poker:

• Although the payouts on the ante bonus are sometimes adjusted as well (4-3-1, 3-2-1, 5-3-1), the net house advantage still hovers between 3.5% to 4.5%.

• Because of the multiple payouts on straights and higher, if you're going to make the ante bet (which isn't recommended), you might as well make the pair plus bet and keep the same call strategy.

• You may see a gimmick where players' tie hands win rather than push on the main bets. This is a good thing. But due to the infrequency of ties, it gives players only a slightly decreased house advantage (just over a tenth of a percentage point better).

• The combination of winning, losing, and tying on the bets and bonuses can be confusing. For instance, let's suppose you bet $10 each on the ante and pair plus. You get a flush and bet another $10 on play, but the dealer turns up a better flush. You'd lose $20, but win $40 and keep your $10 pair plus, for a net of $30. Payouts like this can happen quickly, so make sure you have a solid understanding of how the different scenarios work before sitting down at the table.

"Luck will carry a man across the brook if he is not too lazy to leap."

—*Danish proverb*

Let It Ride was invented in the mid-1990s at the same Shuffle Master company that now owns the rights to Three-Card Poker (described in the previous chapter). It's another single-deck game in which you're dealt three cards. But with this one you're not in direct competition with the dealer—or anyone else, for that matter. You just hope to wind up with a five-card hand that qualifies for the payout schedule (see page 178).

You begin by placing bets of an equal amount on each of the circles.

You begin by placing bets of an equal amount (at least the table minimum) on each of the three betting circles. The Shuffle Master machine deals out three cards to each player and the dealer. The dealer discards one, leaving two common cards facedown. Players are then allowed to look at their hands and in turn indicate if they want to take back the bet from the "1" circle.

> The proper gesture is either a repeated brushing finger motion or scraping card motion against the table and toward yourself. Of course, if you don't want to take back your bet, you can "let it ride."

Once every player has made a decision, the dealer turns up one of the two common cards on the table. Based on this fourth card in their hands, players are given the option to signal a desire to take back the bet from the "2" circle. This decision is made irrespective of the first. In other words, you could take back the first and leave the second, leave the first and take back the second, or take or leave both. After the dealer turns over the second common card, the hands are completed. (There's no taking back that third bet.) Players with less than a pair of tens lose whichever of their bets

remain. Players with at least a pair of tens are paid out
based on this table:

Hand	Payout
Royal flush	1,000 to 1
Straight flush	200 to 1
Four of a kind	50 to 1
Full house	11 to 1
Flush	8 to 1
Straight	5 to 1
Three of a kind	3 to 1
Two pair	2 to 1
Pair of tens or better	1 to 1

Casinos may fiddle around with these numbers, often
lowering the payouts on the higher hands and
sometimes raising them on the lower hands. But based
on this standard schedule and knowing when to take
down your bets or let them ride, the house advantage
for the game is approximately 3.5%.

You should leave up the first bet if your three-card starting hand has:

• A pair of tens or better, or any three of a kind (both automatic winners)

• Three to any straight flush draw, either outside or inside with one card missing.

A pair of tens

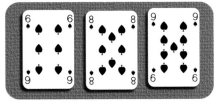

Straight flush draw with one card missing

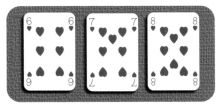

Straight flush draw, outside

You should leave up the second bet if your four-card hand has:

• A pair of tens or better, any three of a kind, or any four of a kind (all automatic winners).

• Four to any flush or straight flush.

• An outside straight draw.

• Any four high cards.

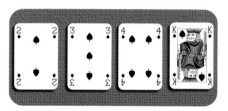

Four to a flush

A winning pair

An outside straight draw

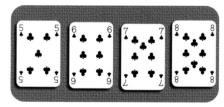

A straight flush draw

Four high cards

Let It Ride also offers a bonus bet for an extra dollar. The return numbers may seem big, but they work out to a scandalous house advantage ranging between 13% and 37%. So even just dropping a dollar at a time with large potential payouts, the bet isn't worth it.

The last thing to keep in mind about this game is that, along with some of the big payouts, it often comes with a restriction on the maximum win per hand—usually between $25,000 and $75,000. If you want to know the most you can bet on each circle and still get paid in full for a royal straight flush (thus not worsening the house edge more than it already is), just divide the maximum payout by 3,000.

"Watch out w'en you'er gittin' all you want. Fattenin
hogs ain't in luck."

—*Joel Chandler Harris (1848–1908), U.S. editor and write*
from Uncle Remus: His Songs and His Saying
"Plantation Proverbs

Optional $1 Progressive
Jackpot Bet

Ante Bet–Any Amount,
Per Table Limits

ANTE

Call Bet–Must Be
2 Times Ante Bet

BET

To play, place a bet in the ante area.

Kentucky native Danny Jones was living in Aruba in the late 1980s when he invented Caribbean Stud Poker. He got a good response by testing it at the Holiday Inn Hotel and Casino, so he marketed the game to cruise ships. His son, Donny, continued to license the game to casinos and thousands of tables sprang up all over the world. In the late 1990s, Mikohn Gaming Corporation bought the game's exclusive worldwide (except for Nevada) distribution rights, along with other progressive games and patents, for $37.5 million. The layout design and payout schedule of Caribbean Stud Poker set the foundation for such other games as Three-Card Poker and Let It Ride. To this day, Caribbean Stud Poker is the most popular proprietary table game.

To play, every player places a bet in the ante area and receives five cards facedown. The dealer also gets five cards, four of which remain facedown and one of which is displayed faceup as a teaser. Players may then either fold (by giving their cards to the dealer, thus losing their ante) or raise (by placing a bet twice their ante in

The dealer needs to have at least ace-king to qualify.

the bet area). The dealer exposes his hand, which needs to contain at least an ace-king to qualify. If it doesn't qualify, the ante bets are paid even money (1 to 1) and the players keep their raise bets. If it does qualify and beats your hand, you lose both bets. If it qualifies and ties your hand—which is rare—neither hand wins and you keep both bets. If your hand beats a qualified dealer hand, you are paid out according to the table below.

Computer simulations have determined that any hand containing a pair of sixes or better has a positive expectation. But if you wait for at least a pair of sixes, you'll fold a bunch of hands you could've won against a

Your Hand	Payout
Royal flush	100 to 1
Straight flush	50 to 1
Four of a kind	20 to 1
Full house	7 to 1
Flush	5 to 1
Straight	4 to 1
Three of a kind	3 to 1
Two pair	2 to 1
One pair or less	1 to 1

Call any hand with at least an ace-king-jack.

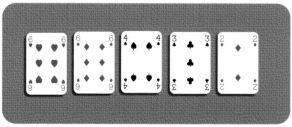

Sixes or better wins a majority of the time.

qualified dealer hand. Therefore, you should call any hand with at least an ace-king-jack. Doing so means you'll forfeit fewer hands and be left with around a 5.3% house advantage.

In-depth mathematical analyses of the game have spawned strategies based on raising with slightly higher hands or if one of your cards matches the dealer's. However, the lowest house advantage any of these analyses has produced is still just over 5.2%. So, don't worry about the dealer's up card, use the ace-king-jack rule of thumb and just accept the fact that the game has a ghastly house edge. Speaking of which, this game does offer another bet, with both a sky-high payout schedule and house advantage. To qualify, you would place a $1 chip in the slot (so it rests halfway in) at the same time you make your ante bet. Before the cards are dealt, the dealer presses a button and the chip drops into a hopper beneath the table. If you make this bet and your hand is at least a flush, you're paid out according to this schedule:

Hand	Payout
Royal Flush	100% of the meter
Straight flush	10% of the meter
Four of a kind	$100–$500
Full house	$75–$250
Flush	$50–$100

The percentage payouts vary according to however high the progressive jackpot is, as indicated by the ever-moving meter. The flat dollar payouts are fixed at each casino, but vary from one casino to the next. The amounts shown are ranges representing typical payouts throughout North America.

Most casinos tend to seed their jackpots with $10,000 to $20,000 and 70 to 75 cents of every $1 side bet. (Some greedy casinos in Las Vegas only add 50 cents on the dollar!) What makes the jackpots build quickly is the fact that multiple tables are linked electronically, enabling players to contribute to and therefore be paid out on a larger shared jackpot. The reason this isn't a smart wager is based on the average bet and seeding rate. In order for the player to even attempt to overcome the built-in 25–30% house advantage on this bet, the progressive would need to be up to between roughly $160,000 and $260,000. Anything less wouldn't represent a full payout based on the odds against the player to make the needed hands.

A few last bits about Caribbean Stud Poker:

• The side bet can't be made without the main bet on your hand. If for some odd reason you were to fold a winning hand, you'd lose both bets and wouldn't be paid anything.

• Caribbean Stud Poker was the first table game to offer a progressive jackpot. It was also the first to accept those bets electronically.

• Danny Jones now lives in Las Vegas and still pursues gaming, but focuses more of his energy on his construction business.

> "Good luck is often with the man who doesn't include it in his plans."
>
> —*Unknown*

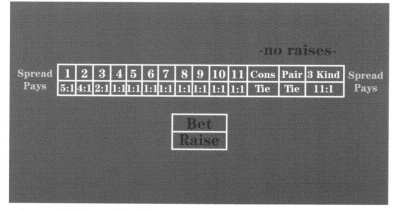

	Spread Pays	1	2	3	4	5	6	7	8	9	10	11	Cons	Pair	3 Kind	Spread Pays
		5:1	4:1	2:1	1:1	1:1	1:1	1:1	1:1	1:1	1:1	1:1	Tie	Tie	11:1	

-no raises-

Bet
Raise

Place your initial wager in the bet area.

This card game, which is also known as "acey-deucey," "between the sheets," and "yablon," found its way into Nevada casinos in the 1980s. It's purely a game of chance—no skill required whatsoever. It's certainly not the most exciting game in the casino, but it might be an interesting diversion . . . in between other games.

As with other games, players begin by placing a wager in the "bet" area. The dealer deals two cards faceup onto the table. If the two cards are consecutive, it's an automatic push (you tie for the hand and get your wager back). If the two cards are the same rank, a third card is dealt. If that card matches the first two, you get paid 11 to 1 on your bet. Otherwise, the hand is a push. In every other situation, the dealer will announce the first two cards' "spread."

> The spread is figured by taking the difference between the two cards' ranks and subtracting one. So the spread between a 9 and 3 would be 5. This reflects the fact that five ranks (4, 5, 6, 7 and 8) are between 3 and 9. The numerical ranks assigned to jack, queen, king, and ace are 11, 12, 13, and 14, respectively. The cards' suits don't matter in this game.

Players are then given an opportunity to double their wager by placing a matching bet in the "raise" area. If the third card dealt is between the first two in rank, players are paid out on (both) their bets according to the schedule printed on the table layout. If the third card is the same as or outside the range of the first two cards, players lose both their bets. Thus, even though aces (always assumed high) and deuces (twos) form the biggest possible spread of 11, it'd be possible to lose if either an ace or deuce were drawn as the third card.

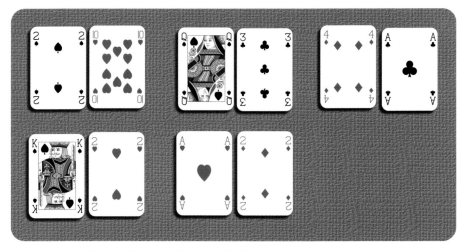

Only raise when the spread is seven or higher, as with these sets of cards.

The smallest spread at which players gain an edge is seven. That's when there are more cards in the deck that could help rather than hurt you. Which, given that there are thirteen different ranks in the deck, is only logical. Thus, only raise when the spread is at least seven (as in the cards shown above). Otherwise, just cross your fingers.

The house advantage for red dog is just under or over 3%, depending on how many decks are used. This house edge falls—somewhat ironically—in between those of most of the other games. In lieu of sharp-minded strategy or fun lights and high jackpots, this might make it interesting to try sometime.

Two last pieces of red dog trivia:

• In this game, the house edge actually decreases (although not by much) as more decks are added!

• There was actually another card game known as "red dog" before this one. In it, players bet on whether they thought any of the five cards from their hand would outrank the next card dealt from the deck. The only proviso was that their card had to be of the same suit as the deck card.

"Don't believe in miracles—depend on them."

—*Laurence J. Peter (1919–1990*
Canadian–U.S. educator and autho

Casino War was just one of the assets purchased from BET Technology by Shuffle Master toward the end of February 2004. With the acquisition, Shuffle Master increased its inventory to almost 3,000 brand-name table games licensed around the world. Of all their table games, Casino War is probably the easiest to play.

After the player bets, the player and dealer are each dealt one card faceup. If the player's card is higher, the player wins 1 to 1 on his bet. If the dealer's card is higher, the player loses the bet.

> Aces are always high, suits don't matter, and since both the player and dealer have the same chance at having the higher card, this is an even proposition so far.

In the off chance that the first cards tie, the player may opt to "go to war." If the player doesn't go to war, he (appropriately termed in this case) "surrenders," forfeiting half his bet. If the player does go to war, he matches his first bet (the dealer also puts up another bet for show). Then three cards are dealt facedown (again

for show) and the player
and dealer each receive
another card faceup.

If the player's second
faceup card either beats
or ties the dealer's second
faceup card, the player
wins 1 to 1 on the second
bet and pushes (nothing
happens) on the first bet.
If the dealer's second card
beats the player's second
card, the player loses
both his bets. The threat
of going to war and
possibly losing two bets
seems like a risky choice,
but this is actually the
smart thing to do.

The house advantage
on surrendering is the
chance that the first two cards will tie multiplied by
how much the player stands to lose. In a single-deck
scenario, three of the fifty-one cards left in the deck
will match the player's first card. And if he surrenders,

Your Cards:

Dealer's Cards:

Player pushes first and wins second.

Your Cards:

Dealer's Cards:

Player loses both bets.

he'll lose half his bet. The product of ⅚₁ and ½ works out to a house edge of 2.94% on surrendering.

The house edge on going to war is a little trickier to calculate, so we'll skip a few insignificant steps along the way. Since the player wins if he and the dealer tie a second time, we first need to look at the chance of tying again. It's not as simple as the first time, because the chance of the same rank tying again (with only two left) and any of the other twelve ranks tying (each with four left) would be different. Combining those two possible ways, the second cards will tie 5.96% of the time. From that figure, we can determine that the player will win 52.98% and the dealer will win 47.02% of the second wars. When the player wins, he wins one unit (the second bet). When the dealer wins, the player loses two units (both bets). Subtracting the likelihood that the player will lose two units from the likelihood that the player will win one unit, and multiplying that difference by the chance that a second war could occur (⅚₁) works out to a house edge of 2.42% on going to war.

If more decks are used, the house advantage for going to war increases to about 3%. The house edge on surrendering increases at an even higher rate. In other words, if you're going to play Casino War, it's always better to go to war when you have the chance.

Your Cards:

Dealer's Cards:

Player pushes first and wins second.

In the rare case that you do tie a second time (as shown at right), some casinos offer a bonus payout on the second bet. Whether they say they're paying double on the second bet and the first bet pushes, triple on the second bet and the first bet loses, or even on both bets, it's all the same net win for you (two units), and it takes away about half a percentage point from the house advantage, bringing the house edge down close to 2%!

Two last points about Casino War:

• If, after reading about the numbers, you still feel squeamish about going to war but like the rest of the action of the game, maybe you should stay home from the casino and just draw for high card with a friend.

• In addition to the main bet, you can also place a wager that the next hand dealt will be a tie. It pays 10 to 1. Unfortunately, with a single deck, the odds of a tie occurring are 16 to 1. That makes for a wallet-busting 35.29% house advantage! It goes down to about half that with more decks, but that still leaves it way above any bet you should come close to considering.

"Be ready when opportunity comes . . . Luck is the time when preparation and opportunity meet."
—*Roy D. Chapin Jr. (1915–2001), Chairman, American Motors Corporation*

The video poker concept is simple: put in from one to five coins; hit the "deal/draw" button; hit the "hold" button to keep none, some, or all of your cards; hit the "deal/draw" button again; and get paid if you wind up with at least a certain poker hand. To the casual observer, it may seem like just another slot machine.

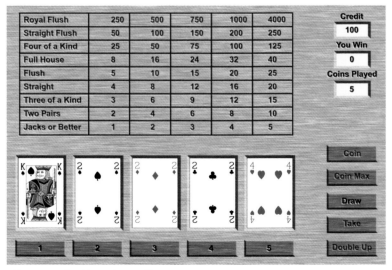

Royal Flush	250	500	750	1000	4000	**Credit** 100
Straight Flush	50	100	150	200	250	
Four of a Kind	25	50	75	100	125	**You Win** 0
Full House	8	16	24	32	40	
Flush	5	10	15	20	25	**Coins Played**
Straight	4	8	12	16	20	5
Three of a Kind	3	6	9	12	15	
Two Pairs	2	4	6	8	10	
Jacks or Better	1	2	3	4	5	

The screen of a video poker machine

Payout per Number of Coins Played

Hand	1	2	3	4	5
Royal flush	250	500	750	1,000	4,000
Straight flush	50	100	150	200	250
Four of a kind	25	50	75	100	125
Full house	9	18	27	36	45
Flush	6	12	18	24	30
Straight	4	8	12	16	20
Three of a kind	3	6	9	12	15
Two pair	2	4	6	8	10
Jacks or better	1	2	3	4	5

You sit down, play by yourself at your own pace, and hope to win a giant payout. But unlike with slots, it's possible to know how good a video poker machine is just by looking at it and use skill to gain a long-term advantage over the casino!

To judge whether a video poker machine is worthy of your business, walk up to the table—the payout table, that is, such as the typical one shown above for "jacks or better."

Since the machine takes your money at the start of each hand, all payouts are by definition "for 1," rather than "to 1." This means that a payout of at least one unit is required to break even on any particular hand.

This particular table is known as the game's "full pay" version, since it's the most common jacks or better payout schedule and gives a decent return. It's specifically identified as a "9/6," based on the ratio between the one-coin payouts for a full house (9 for 1) and a flush (6 for 1). In some casinos, you'll often find otherwise-identical games with different payout tables right next to each other! Here's a comparison of the most frequent jacks or better tables:

Jacks or Better Payout Schedules

Full House/Flush	Percentage Return	House Advantage
9/7	100.80%	-0.80%
10/6	100.70%	-0.70%
9/6	99.54%	0.46%
8/6	98.39%	1.61%
8/5	97.30%	2.70%
7/5	96.15%	3.85%
6/5	95.00%	5.00%

As you can see, by slightly altering the payouts on the full house and flush, it greatly changes the return for the player. If the range of almost six percentage points (between the 9/7 and 6/5 tables) doesn't seem like a lot, consider the fact it's more than the difference between playing and not playing most of the games so far in this book! Needless to say, before sitting down to any machine, you should shop around. As a rule, you don't want to play jacks or better if it offers less than 9 for 1 on the full house or less than 6 for 1 on a flush.

You very much do, however, want payouts of higher than 9 or 6 on those hands. If you can find them, these machines actually pay out more than 100%! What this means is that in the long run, you, the player, could actually have an advantage over the casino. But—and you knew there had to be a "but"—it's based on always playing five coins with solid strategy until you hit a royal flush.

The reason the royal flush is so important is that it's not only the best hand with the highest payout, but has the only payout that's disproportionate to the increasing number of coins. In other words, whether a straight pays you four for playing one coin or twenty for playing five coins, it's the same ratio. The royal pays 250 on one coin, but much more than 1,250 on five coins. So you can still do fine by playing "short-coin" (less than the five-coin maximum) in video poker. You're just not likely to get that edge over the casino in the long run.

Once you know which machine to sit down at, you've conquered half the battle. The other half—actually playing the game well—is where skill comes in. After all, the casino isn't in business to make it easy for you to win money from them. Fortunately, over the past few decades, ever since video poker first came along, experts have analyzed the best ways to play every possible starting hand. Certain plays may be obvious, such as always holding:

- The three cards of a three of a kind

- The four cards of a two pair

- All five cards of any straight flush

- All five for four of a kind

- All five for a full house

The reason to keep all five with a four of a kind is that, without wild cards, the hand can't be improved by drawing a card.

Holding three of a kind

Holding two pair

Holding a pat straight flush

Holding a pat four of a kind

Holding a pat full house

It's good to keep most pat straights.

It's also good to keep most pat flushes.

But not every "pat" hand (one that is already a winner) is necessarily better than every "drawing" hand (one that needs other cards to be a winner). For instance, it's good to keep most pat straights and flushes (as shown left). But with a hand like 9♣, 10♥, J♥, Q♥, and K♥, it makes sense to break up the straight by ditching the nine for a chance at the big payout on the royal flush. In this case, even if you don't make the royal, you'll still have a good shot at a regular flush, another straight, or at the very least a pair of jacks or better.

In other words, simply knowing the rules and rankings of five-card draw poker (upon which jacks or better is based) won't take you far enough. In order to get the optimal return on a particular machine (i.e., 99.54% on a 9/6), you'd have to play perfect strategy based on the rankings of over three dozen differently quantified types of starting hands.

Every starting hand's correct play is based on comparing all the potential payouts by keeping certain cards, multiplying the odds of making a particular hand by what the payout would be if it hit, and adding together those potential payouts when multiple winning hands are possible.

A simplified version of the proper guidelines can get you within about a tenth of a percentage point for the return on optimal play. The key is making the right decisions when multiple potential hands are possible within the same five starting cards. For instance, when given the option, you should choose:

> 1. Four cards to a royal flush over a pat flush (as in A♠, K♠, J♠, 10♠, 4♠) or straight, but a pat straight (as in 5♦, 6♦, 7♦, 8♦, 9♥) or flush over any other straight flush draw.

> 2. A high pair (jacks or better) over any other drawing hand unless it's four to a straight flush (as in 8♣, 9♣, 10♣, J♣, J♦).

> 3. A high pair (as in 7♣, Q♠, Q♦, K♦, A♦) over three to a royal flush.

> 4. Three to a royal flush (as in A♣, Q♣, 10♣, 6♣, 3♥) over four to a regular flush.

> 5. Four to a regular flush over a low pair (tens or less).

Hold the flush draw, not the pair.

Keep the low pair, not the straight draw.

6. A low pair over four to an outside straight.

7. Four to an outside straight (as in 8♣, 9♦, 10♥, J♠, K♠) over two suited high cards.

8. Two suited high cards (as in Q♣, K♣, 2♥, 3♥, 4♥) over three to a straight flush.

9. Three to a straight flush (as in 5♦, 9♠, 10♠, J♠, K♥) over two unsuited high cards.

10. Only two unsuited high cards from more than two (as in 4♦, 7♠, J♥, Q♣, A♦), since keeping extras only hurts your chances at a qualifying pair.

11. One high card, if that's all you have (as in K♦, 9♣, 8♠, 4♦, 2♥).

12. To get rid of all five in the absence of pairs, high cards, or worthwhile drawing hands (as with an abysmal hand like 2♣, 3♠, 6♥, 9♦, 10♠). In contrast, at least with cards of the same suit, you can draw to a flush.

Note that the above rules are transitive. In other words, if hand A is better than hand B and hand B is better than hand C, then hand A is better than hand C. To put it another way, since rule 6 is higher on the list than rule 7, you know that it'd be better to keep a low pair (as in 7♥, 7♠, 9♦, K♣, Q♣) than two suited high cards. This may seem counterintuitive, given the number of sevens versus kings and queens that could help your hand in each scenario!

Now that you know what to do, here are two prime examples of what not to do, based on common mistakes:

Hold a high pair.

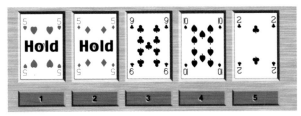

Hold a low pair.

A salvageable flush draw

Payout Ratio on:

"Full Pay" Machine	Full House/Flush	Payout Percentage
Deuces wild	9/5*	100.76%
Jokers wild	7/5	100.65%
Double bonus	10/7	100.17%
Double double bonus	10/6	100.07%
Aces and eights	8/5	99.78%
Jacks or better	9/6	99.54%
Tens or better	6/5	99.14%
Deuces and jokers wild	9/6**	99.07%

*Ratio of straight flush/four of a kind
**Ratio of five of a kind/straight flush

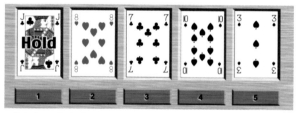

Only keep the jack.

• Never keep four to an inside straight (see left). Only keep the jack.

• Never keep a "kicker" (a high card you're hoping to pair up). It only hurts your chances for improving. Only keep the queens. Or only keep the sevens (see right).

Never keep a kicker (the ace), only keep the queens.

Deuces: Payout per Number of Coins Played

Hand	1	2	3	4	5
Natural royal flush	250	500	750	1,000	4,000
Four deuces	200	400	600	800	1,000
Wild royal flush	25	50	75	100	125
Five of a kind	15	30	45	60	75
Straight flush	9	18	27	36	45
Four of a kind	5	10	15	20	25
Full house	3	6	9	12	15
Flush	2	4	6	8	10
Straight	2	4	6	8	10
Three of a kind	1	2	3	4	5

While jacks or better is certainly a favorite, you'll find fleets of other video poker games among the seemingly endless banks of machines: tens or better, aces and eights,

Only hold the sevens.

double bonus, double double bonus, deuces wild, jokers wild, deuces and jokers wild . . . the list goes on and on. And although they may sound similar, certain games' "full pay" schedules are better than others (see table on page 206).

As you can see, you can't judge a table purely by the numbers. A 7/5 doesn't necessarily indicate an awful machine, just as a 9/6 doesn't necessarily signify a great one. Each game is different and requires its own optimal strategy. We won't get into every single one here, but we will look at the most popular game with wild cards, deuces wild—which also just happens to boast the top payout percentage in the above table. A typical expanded full ("9/5") payout schedule for deuces can be seen on page 207.

From this table, it is clear the minimum paying hand is now a couple of notches higher. Straights and flushes have the same payout. Four deuces and five of a kind are added to the mix. And there's a distinction between getting a wild royal flush (using wild deuces) and a natural royal (without using any deuces).

Since wild twos can represent any card you want, rule number one in this game is, quite simply, to never discard a deuce! Rule number two—which you'll see emphasized throughout—is to always keep any pat royal flush you're dealt, whether it's wild or not.

After those two rules, the game's strategy is broken down and defined by how many twos your opening hand contains. Again, since perfect strategy quantifies about five dozen different starting hands, the below simplified version—which shaves only a fraction of a

percentage point off the
expected return—should
work fine for the average
player:

Keep any pat royal flush, whether it is wild or not.

> When dealt four deuces,
> keep all five cards. (Keep
> in mind rule number
> one: it is impossible to
> improve your payout by
> only drawing one.)

Based on this rule, you'd
keep all five for a hand
like 10♠, 2♠, 2♦, 2♥, 2♣.
Although it could be

Break up the straight flush for a royal draw.

considered five tens or a wild royal flush, the only hand
that counts is the highest possible. In this case, you
would get paid on the four deuces, a junior jackpot
that tends to "cycle" (hit once in) about every 5,000
hands.

> When dealt three deuces:

> 1. Keep any pat royal (both the other cards
> would have to be 10 or higher and suited).

> 2. Keep four to a royal (if only one of the
> other cards is a 10 or higher), even if you
> have to break up a straight flush.

3. Only keep five of a kind 10 or higher (such as 2♥, 2♦, 2♠, Q♠, Q♣). Get rid of nines or less based on the fact that more high cards are left in the deck available to make a royal.

4. If you have a regular straight flush (with less than four to a royal), a straight flush draw, or any lesser (made or drawing) hand, keep only the three deuces. The chances for a payoff on four deuces, a royal, five of a kind, or a four of a kind (the lowest possible hand you can make with three wild cards) make breaking up any otherwise strong hands worth it.

Only keep the deuces.

When dealt two deuces:

1. Keep any pat straight flush or royal flush.

2. Keep four to a royal and four to a regular straight flush if the two other cards are suited connectors six or higher, even if it breaks up a made flush or straight. With two deuces, at least a six as your lowest suited

Break up the flush for the straight flush draw.

connector maximizes the number of cards that can make you a straight flush. In this case, a same-suited three, four, five, eight, nine, ten, or either of the other two deuces (eight cards in total) will do it.

Keep only the deuces, despite the straight made and straight flush draw.

3. Keep any five of a kind.

4. With four of a kind, draw one to the possible five of a kind.

5. If a hand isn't at least a four of a kind or a qualifying straight flush draw, keep just the pair of deuces.

Hold onto just the pair of deuces.

When dealt only one deuce:

1. Keep any pat royal, straight flush, five of a kind, or full house.

2. Draw one to four of a kind.

3. Keep any pat straight or flush,

Ignore the straight and flush draws, keep the deuces.

It's best to keep the flush here.

unless you also have four cards to a royal (as in 9♣, 2♠, J♠, Q♠, K♠), or four to a regular straight flush, if three of the nonwild cards are suited, consecutive, and five or higher (as in 2♠, 5♦, 6♦, 7♦, J♥). Again, this maximizes the number of cards that can make a straight flush. Since the three suited cards in the hand shown above are nonconsecutive, it's better to keep the flush.

4. Draw two to three of a kind.

5. Keep three to a royal, unless you also have four to any other straight flush (as in 5♦, 8♥, 2♠, 10♥, J♥).

6. In the absence of any of the above hands, keep three to a straight flush if you have two suited connectors six or higher (as in 2♥, 7♣, 8♣, J♥, K♦). Since the hand shown below doesn't qualify with either the seven-nine or three-four, you'd keep only the two.

7. If none of these conditions is met (as with the three- and four-card straight, flush, and straight flush draws), keep just the deuce.

Only keep the two here.

When dealt no deuces:

Ignore the pat straight and go for the royal.

1. Keep any pat royal.

2. Keep any other pat hand listed in the payout table, unless you have four to a royal (see top right).

Ignore the pair and keep three to the royal.

3. Keep a pair unless you have at least three cards to a royal (see right, upper middle) or four to a regular straight flush (see right). You should ignore four-card draws to regular straights and flushes when you have a pair. If you have two pair, only keep one pair. The other two cards (as with all kickers) only hurt your chances to make the minimum three of a kind payout.

Go for the straight flush draw.

The flush draw works fine.

Keep three to the straight flush.

Ignore the straight draw, keep the pair.

Ignore the flush draw, keep the pair.

With no better draws, keep the suited 10-jack.

4. Without a pair, keep four to a flush or outside straight. If a hand has both (as in 6♥, 7♥, 8♠, 9♥, Q♥), keep either equal-valued four-card draw.

5. Without a four-card flush or outside straight draw, keep three to any straight flush (see top).

6. Only keep four to an inside straight if no better drawing hand (mentioned above) is possible and a two isn't the missing card. So, for a hand like A♦, 3♠, 4♥, 5♣, 9♠, get rid of all five cards.

7. In lieu of any other better drawing hands, only keep a ten-jack, ten-queen, or jack-queen suited (as in 3♣, 6♥, 9♠, 10♦, Q♦).

So, you shouldn't keep any other two suited (as in A♣, J♣, 8♦, 7♠, 3♥) or nonsuited high-card combinations. You also shouldn't keep three to an outside or inside straight, regardless of whether a three-card flush draw is present; and you certainly shouldn't keep a hand like the one on page 216, bottom.

In about 20% of the hands in deuces wild, it's best to get rid of all five cards to make room for more possibilities. (By comparison, that's about seven times more often than those playing jacks or better should get rid of their entire hand.)

The trick to learning all these rules is to pay more attention to the

Don't keep high nonsuited cards.

Don't keep three to an outside straight.

Don't keep three to an inside straight.

Don't keep these cards, even when a three-card flush is present.

A three-card flush, but don't keep these cards.

Definitely get rid of this sort of hand.

rules that don't make immediate sense to you.

Like other video poker games, deuces wild offers good potential returns in the long run, but can have big swings in the action in the short run. To ride them out, you need to maintain the strategies described here. These strategies can't be applied directly to other games, even if they are similar—jokers wild uses a fifty-three-card deck with one wild card, so it needs to be played very differently from deuces wild.

You can't expect to do well by choosing any machine at random and just playing with common sense. In addition to the strategic mistakes you're likely to make, you may receive weaker payouts based on several other factors.

We've already shown that the same game could offer a different payout schedule for the same hands. But, it's also possible that the same game could require different hands for the same minimum payout. For instance, needing two pair versus kings or better to receive a 1 for 1 payout in jokers wild. Some jacks or better machines offer different payouts on a four of a kind with aces, twos through fours, and fives or higher.

Progressive Jackpots

Another big factor in the same game offering different payouts is whether or not it has a progressive jackpot (pooled electronically between many machines). In terms of both direct dollars and overall percentage, these machines tend to pay out lower. But it is possible to get over a 100% return. It all depends on how high the meter gets in relation to the particular payout table. As a rule of thumb, the break-even point tends to be 8,750 times the denomination. In other words, $8,750 on a dollar machine, just under $2,200 on a quarter machine, and $440 on a nickel machine. Anything higher than these figures represents an advantage for the player.

Nickels vs. Quarters vs. Dollars

The denomination of a machine (nickel, quarter, $1, $5, etc.) also affects your potential winnings. Higher denominations tend to be better because they usually offer better payout schedules. The casino knows that they'll retain fewer wagers, but the ones they do retain will be higher. You might typically find a quarter machine offers a 9/6, whereas the nickel version offers an 8/5.

Shop Around

Geography can play a part in the payout from video poker machines. For example, the machines in downtown Las Vegas (away from the Strip) tend to be better. That's because they cater to the competitive local market, consisting of video poker aficionados.

In the end, video poker is about making the right decisions: in terms of the game chosen, the table offered, and the strategy employed, but also in how quickly you can play each hand correctly. If you're playing a game with a potential player advantage, you want to squeeze in as many well-played hands per hour as possible. After all, the more hands you play, the higher your likelihood of getting the top payout (and therefore approximating the game's overall optimal payout). If you consider the fact that a royal flush might occur once in every 40,000 to 70,000 hands, that could translate to anywhere from 70 to 100 hours of play. During that time, here's some perspective on how much bad decisions could cost you: Consider the fact that playing five quarters per hand ($1.25) at the relatively slow rate of 400 hands per hour, which would give you a "coin in" (amount of money you're putting in play) of $500 an hour. That means that for every percentage point you give up by choosing the wrong machine or playing improper strategy, you're burning $5 an hour. That can really add up, keeping in mind the percentage point spread in most machines mentioned earlier (almost six) and the number of hours you might play in a session. While video poker may offer an edge, it takes as much patience as skill to reap the rewards.

Video Poker: Things to Bear in Mind

• The random number generator that determines your hand actually selects ten cards at a time, giving you five for your starting hand and five others to possibly replace them. However, each hand is played independently, so you could see the same card in consecutive hands.

• Although with most games you indicate which cards to hold, with some you select which to discard. So when you first sit down to play, double-check to make sure which kind it is!

• Multistrike poker allows you to play additional hands with increasing payouts (up to eight times the normal amount) when you win consecutive hands. Despite the fact that the game may automatically tell you which cards to hold, stick to your best strategies, select the right cards manually (if necessary), and you could increase your winnings—to around 99.8% on a 9/6 jacks or better, for instance.

"Fortune cannot be flattered by such fetish worship. But she can be wooed and won by hard work"

—*William Maxwell Beaverbrook (1879–1964),*

English publisher

SLOTS

In the late 1890s in San Francisco, German-born mechanic, inventor, and entrepreneur Charles August Fey created the predecessor to today's modern slot machine, the "Liberty Bell." It required a nickel to play and had three wheels set in motion by a spring-loaded lever. The ten symbols that whizzed by on each wheel consisted of hearts, diamonds, spades, horseshoes, and liberty bells, particular combinations of which would pay out money.

Several years later, the demand was high—both from patrons and other manufacturers looking to get in on the game. But Fey refused to work with other vendors. Some suspect that in 1905, the Mills Novelty Company of Chicago replicated a machine from a San Francisco saloon and in 1906 began marketing it under the same name and design. That same year, the Great San Francisco Earthquake and Fire of 1906 destroyed Fey's slot machine factory.

Mills went on to make a few important design changes. For instance, they increased the number of symbols per wheel to twenty, which made for a

1-in-8,000-chance jackpot. Creating a transparent coin reservoir allowed the physical payout to be visible to the player—and the fact that metal slugs weren't being used in place of coins to the machine's operator. With an expanded main view window, the new machine offered patrons a glimpse of near-payoffs, giving rise to the psychological fallacy of a machine being "close" to paying out, a fallacy that lives on to this day.

A few years later, in order to skirt laws against gambling machines that paid out money, manufacturers attempted to disguise their "one-armed bandits" as vending machines by incorporating gum and candy as payouts. The playing card–based symbols gave way to "bar" symbols (still used today) signifying candy. The orange, pear, cherry, and lemon symbols that reflected the gum flavors inside are why slots are known as "fruit machines" in Britain.

Slot machines proliferated through Prohibition. Bugsy Siegel brought them into his Flamingo Hotel in Las Vegas, supposedly as a way of entertaining the high rollers' wives and girlfriends—hopefully not right next to each other! Progress slowed in the 1950s when the Johnson Act banned slots from all states without legalized gambling. It took decades for them to regain their momentum. By the 1990s, a century after they'd

been created, slot machines surpassed table games both in popularity and revenue for the casinos. Currently, slot machines are outlawed in California, except on tribal reservations. Those properties are limited to having a maximum of 2,000 machines; pending state legislation may increase that number.

As opposed to the simple designs of yesterday, today's slot machines are complicated creatures. They still require no skill to play. Just put your money in, pull the lever—or even easier, press the button—and hope that a winning combination of symbols winds up on the payline. But some of the video slots (which increasingly dominate the old-fashioned variety) have as many as five, seven, or even nine (animated) reels; hundreds of symbols; and up to twenty-one different paylines! Fortunately, these video-based games also come with a "help" screen to explain how it all works.

You don't automatically get paid by the paylines. You have to first pay for them in order to make them active. For instance, if you choose a four-reel nickel machine with fifteen payout lines, it will cost 75 cents per spin to make them all active. Of course, you could just play the same game with fewer paylines, but then you have to choose which and how many—not to mention the fact that you could be faced with the psychological trauma of "missing" a payout on an inactive line. It's probably better all around to play a game with fewer reels in the first place.

To give you an idea of how dramatically increasing the number of reels affects your chances, imagine three reels with twenty symbols per reel. If you added twenty more symbols per reel (assuming, for the sake of argument, that each symbol represents one stop on the reel), that would yield $40 \times 40 \times 40 = 64,000$ stops. If you added just one more twenty-symbol reel (all other things being equal), that would yield $20 \times 20 \times 20 \times 20 = 160,000$ stops. That's more than twice as many—and it goes up exponentially with more reels. The jackpots may be higher on machines with more reels, but the chances of actually hitting any of them plunge.

The size and odds against hitting a jackpot are even higher when a machine is a "progressive." That could either mean that a particular slot machine has a variable jackpot or that a series of machines in the casino, dozens around town, or even hundreds throughout the state are all linked electronically to build and eventually pay out a variable jackpot. If no one hits one of those big ones, after a while it can climb into the millions, approaching payoffs the size of state-run lotteries! As with the lotteries, those gigantic payouts are both heavily taxed and generally doled out over a period of years. You can tell the difference between single- and multiple-machine progressives because the latter tend to be grouped together and are topped by flashy electronic meters that all read the same (changing) amount.

In the olden days, a large team of "slot professionals" could gang up against a progressive with a jackpot that outweighed the odds against hitting it. For example, a top prize of more than $8,000 on a machine with three reels of twenty symbols each. However, with the technology involved today, not even a large slot team with a huge bankroll could make a meaningful dent against a modern megaprogressive jackpot.

If you're looking for better odds on a slot machine, stick with the "flat tops" or "straight slots" that have a fixed jackpot. The jackpots may be smaller, but those machines tend to have a higher hit frequency and payout percentage. Some pay as much as 99% or even over 100% back—as with video poker, this is based on hitting the highest payout at some point. Unfortunately, they may be few and far between. And unlike with video poker, there's no way of walking up to the average machine, looking at it, and knowing what the estimated percentage return is. The best you can do is find one where playing the maximum amount of coins (usually two or three) gives you a worthwhile disproportionate payoff. If the jackpot when playing three coins is only one-and-a-half times as much as when playing two (i.e., 3,000 to 2,000), look for another machine. But if it's at least twice as high (i.e., 4,000 to 2,000), that's a good sign.

Since some casinos offer machines based on a minimum ranging from one penny to $500 per spin, you need to begin by shopping around for the right denomination of slots for you. (They tend to be grouped together by denomination, with ones higher than $5 in a private VIP area.) It makes no sense to find a fabulous payout ratio on a $5 machine when you have no intention of putting in $10 or $15 per spin. Play the highest denomination at which you feel comfortable playing the maximum number of coins per spin (again, given a worthy top payout), since the higher-denomination machines usually pay out at a higher percentage.

If you're not sure how much per spin is right for you, you might want to try a multidenominational slot, one that offers different minimum bets and pays out paper vouchers instead of coins (since the coin amounts vary).

Based on data from around the country, the percentage of return for nickel to $5 machines tends to average between around 92% and 96%, respectively. That makes 6% the overall average house edge on lower-limit slots. But in practice, they might range anywhere from 83% to 99%—that's a big swing! As with video poker, the slot machines in the less-glitzy downtown Las Vegas establishments tend to pay out higher than those on the Strip. It's also been noted that for some reason the slots on the East Coast pay slightly less on average than in other parts of the country.

Faithful slot players continue their search for the "loosest" slots (with the best payouts), which is why many places advertise having them. Better slots do exist, but unless you see signage certifying that a particular machine is set to pay at a particular rate (at least 98%), don't believe the hype. The casino could just be announcing that one of their slots somewhere (they won't tell you where) offers a high rate of return.

Wherever the machines are, nowadays computer chips are at the brains of their operation, continuously generating a series of random numbers. The very instant you pull the lever or hit the button, it selects some of those random numbers, processes them, and maps them to particular stops (some of which don't have symbols) on each reel. In other words, the reels' spinning is just for show, a callback to when the speed of the reels affected the outcome. The computer knows if your spin is a winner before the reels come to rest on any of the scores of possible positions.

At the Silver Legacy Casino in Reno toward the end of 2000, actuary-turned-gambling-expert Michael Shackleford—better known as the "Wizard of Odds"— experimented with thousands of spins at a particular 25-cent machine over a five-day period and found that certain stops on each wheel appeared to be weighted. In other words, some symbols/spaces consistently came up more often than others, especially more than ones linked to higher payouts. That doesn't imply that machines are cheating players out of payouts. States have regulatory gaming bureaus that randomly field-test machines to make sure the chips are set to pay out what they're supposed to. What Shackleford's work does mean is that every combination doesn't necessarily have the same chance of appearing. Thus, simply multiplying the number of stops on each reel might not be a good measure of how likely a particular payout is.

Of course, the likeliest payout is for the house, which makes billions of dollars a year from slots. Because these machines, on average, account for more than two-thirds of casino revenue, casinos will do whatever they can to draw your attention and lure you in. You might first notice bright flashing lights around a payout table, hear the clanging of coins hitting the metal tray, see an amusing graphic dancing across the video monitor, or even be coaxed in by a synthesized human voice. Upon further inspection, you're likely to find a machine based on a familiar movie, TV show, board game, or any of a variety of other brands—anything that seems friendly and fun and gets you to sit down.

Once engaged, that's where the casino pulls out all the stops. You don't have to continuously feed coins in, you can submit bills. (Whether credit and debit cards should be accepted is a highly contested argument.)

You don't have to strain yourself by pulling the lever or pressing multiple buttons, just the "bet max" button will set the reels in motion each time. Some games placate players by offering gimmicky buttons such as "nudge" or "hold" that purport to have an effect on the outcome, but really don't. When you do win, you're given credits so that you don't have to refeed money into the machine and can just play until it's gone—certain side games either give you a bonus play or chance to "parlay your wins." Unfortunately, the latter is a good way to quickly lose back your bet. In fact, slot players tend to give up more than 50 percent of what they feed in, often because they or someone they know hit a big payout on that type of machine in the past. Or perhaps they just don't know when to get up and walk away. The result is simple: the more money that gets wagered, the more the casino profits.

Because the casinos profit so much, they attempt to compensate the folks who feed their cash cows the most. One way is by offering a guaranteed cash rebate on a certain percentage of players' losses. They can well afford to do this, but they'll only do it for members of their slot club. If you plan to be a "slot junkie" (consistent player), then it makes sense to join a slot club.

To get started, go to a special desk in the casino, sign up, and they will give you a plastic card with a magnetic strip on the back. Insert the card into a special card reader at whatever slot machine you play (or present it to the dealer at a table game). The casino is able to track which brands and denominations of machines you play at, your average bet, duration of play, and how much you wager overall.

Based on those figures—not whether you win or lose—casinos offer a wide range of incentives to their best customers: access to lounges, complimentary meals, free rooms, tickets to shows, discounts to shops on the premises, invitations to special events, free entry to slot tournaments, and even birthday gifts. In this era of conglomerated corporations, sometimes you can earn and redeem points within a certain group of sister casinos, such as with the MGM Mirage (Bellagio, New York New York, Treasure Island, Mirage, and the MGM) or Park Place (Caesars Palace, Bally's, Paris, Flamingo, and Hilton) properties. As with airline miles, it's best to find one group that serves your needs best and accrue as many points as possible with it. But shop around before you sign up for any old slot program—casinos are willing to compete for your business. Hey, as long as you're going to risk money, you might as well be rewarded!

Great Slot Machine Myths

1. A certain (brand of) machine always pays out better. And if you bribe the change clerks with a few bucks, they'll tell you which. First off, the computer chip inside that controls everything doesn't care what brand is plastered on the outside. And second, if the change clerks making just over minimum wage roving the floor had access to information like that, do you think they'd be change clerks?

2. If you get up from a machine and someone sits down and hits a jackpot on the next spin, you would've won. Not at all likely, unless you'd set the reels spinning at the exact same fraction of an instant the other person did. Any other moment in time would've generated a different series of random numbers and been keyed to a different outcome. Still, people are serious about "their" machines and you should always ask someone sitting next to a machine you want to play if the one you want is available.

3. How warm/cold or new/old a coin is says something about how close a payoff is. Sorry, all it says is that the lights inside the machine are hot and you're reading too much into the whole process.

4. A machine that hasn't hit big in a while is "due." Unfortunately for the bankrolls of many players, the payout return percentages are calculated over extended periods of time, over hundreds of thousands of spins, long after true believers of this credo will have bankrupted. On the opposite side of the coin, just because a machine hits a big payout doesn't mean it couldn't do it again soon.

5. The casino places better machines near the doors or at the ends of aisles. This seems plausible because those machines are more visible, but it isn't true. Which doesn't mean the ones closest the entrance and on the corners are bad machines.

6. Machines pay out more if a slot club card isn't used. The card readers and chips that determine the outcomes are part of different mechanisms. Besides, casinos don't want to punish their best customers. Think about it. If someone hit huge on a certain machine, they'd be likely to come back for life. Any casino would love a customer like that!

7. If you win a lot of money in a particular session, the casino will report you to the IRS. It doesn't go by the session, but the spin. If on any pull you win more than $1,200, the casino will report it to the IRS. You're on your honor to report your net wins over the year. That's why you should always keep a log of your wins and losses. If you hit it big, your losses could help to mitigate any taxes owed. By the way, whereas smaller jackpots are paid directly by the machine, larger ones activate a light on top of the machine that notifies an employee to come over and pay you in person.

If you've been playing at one particular machine for a while, check every so often to make sure that the card machine is working. Barring any technical glitches (which do happen), you want it to track all of your play.

Slots are interesting in that the most experienced players are no bigger experts than beginners. They may know more about when certain deals are (for accruing points at a higher rate) or which casinos treat their slot players better. But in the absence of skill—especially in tournaments—anything else is just luck and hearsay. In fact, if slot junkies are more of anything, they're more superstitious! You'll see them holding or wearing lucky charms, inserting coins or pressing the spin button in a ritualistic way . . . anything to try to please the mysterious, unpredictable powers that be so that fortune will smile on them. Statistically, it only takes one big win per lifetime to validate all this craziness.

Unlike with video poker, speed is not your friend with slots. You want to slow down your play. Go through the motions. Cash out every once in a while and only redeposit some of the coins. Also, set strict limits on how long you plan to play and how much you're willing to lose. Most importantly, never play with money you can't afford to lose. That means you need to be honest with yourself. Don't talk yourself

"Cash Lost in Me"

• If you're playing with a cup of coins, keep it on your lap so you'd know if someone grabbed it. Often, thieves will try to get you to look the other way by flicking a coin onto the floor nearby. If the cup is resting just out of your reach, it's an easy snatch for them.

• Never abandon or continue playing on a machine that doesn't finish paying you. If it runs out of money or has a malfunction, press the attendant button and let an employee help you. As soon as you walk away, someone else can claim they were sitting there when the jackpot hit. If you were to put in another coin, it would ruin the evidence of the previous incomplete payout.

• At the end of each session, bring your cup of coins—or the paper printouts some casinos use to indicate how much money you left the machine with—to the cage and exchange it for bills. It's a step to keep you from continuously playing and losing more than you have to.

• Just remember, the letters in the words "slot machines" can be rearranged to form the phrase "cash lost in me!"

into playing till your money's all gone. Cash out, get up, and walk away. Heck, you can always come back! And finally, try not to get too serious about the whole process. It's supposed to be entertainment, after all. So be civil to others—no slot machine is worth fighting over just so you can lose your money!

"What helps luck is a habit of watching for opportunities, of having a patient but restless mind, of sacrificing one's ease or vanity, of uniting a love of detail to foresight, and of passing through hard times bravely and cheerfully."

—*Victor Cherbuliez (1829–1899), French novelist*

KENO

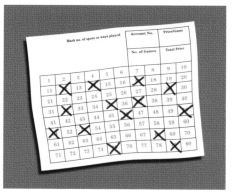

Keno ticket

Thousands of years ago in China, a lottery was created as a way to get citizens to contribute more to a war effort.

Centuries later, the game traveled to the United States with the many immigrant Chinese railroad and mine workers in the mid-1800s. The characters of the "Chinese lottery," as it came to be known, were eventually replaced with numbers to entice more English-speaking Americans to play. Although many other forms of gambling were made legal in Nevada, lotteries were not. So the game's moniker was transformed into "horse race keno." (Traces of this iteration still survive today in that each game is known as a "race," presumably of certain numbers to be picked.) Not long after, to avoid a Nevada off-track betting tax, the game's name was shortened to "keno," as it is known today.

All the while, the keno concept has remained simple: From a pool of possibilities, players pick a certain number of symbols. Depending on how many come up, winners get paid a particular amount. In this case, the pool consists of the numbers 1 through 80. Players may select a group as big as twenty "spots." And the various payouts for how many of the chosen spots "catch" (are drawn) are set by each casino.

What each casino's brochure of keno payout tables won't tell you is that the house advantage for this game is consistently between 25% and 35% (plus or minus 5%). If that range looks like tax bracket percentages, just remember the game's origin!

This huge house edge gives them reason enough to make keno very convenient to play. While there's a keno lounge where the action actually takes place, you can play from any part of the casino—while you play other games, eat, sit by the pool, even sleep!

Your first option is to visit the keno lounge, where you'll find plenty of tickets. To fill one out, use one of the official crayons to put an X through between one and twenty numbers (some casinos allow a maximum group of fifteen to be chosen). For a ticket such as a "fourteen-spot," where it says to mark the number of spots, you'd write "1/14." The price per game is whatever you want, based on a minimum usually between 25 cents and $2. The number of games allows you to play the same numbers for between two and a thousand consecutive races. Based on multiplying your price per game by the number of games, you fill in the total amount of your wager and bring the wager and ticket to the "writer" (dealer) at the counter.

The writer will confirm the numbers you picked by making you a copy or giving you a printout and keeping the original, which is important for verification purposes. It's possible to follow the "call" of each game on the big "board" (display) in the lounge, video monitors positioned throughout the casino, and often on a special TV channel in your room. If you win anything, you generally have until the next game starts to collect. The casino wants closure on each drawing, so you need to quickly get back to the writer and hand in your printout or ticket copy.

You'll get paid and they may ask you if you want to play the same numbers again, which you may want to do based on either superstition or expediency. (You can also replay your or others' losing tickets.) For the multirace tickets, you don't have to go back after each race if you win, which is how you can play in your sleep.

To play while elsewhere in the casino, you need to flag down a "runner." This is a casino employee specifically servicing the keno game who walks around the casino—appropriately enough—saying the word "Keno." If you don't catch their eye by waving to them, just give a shout of "Keno!" to grab their attention. They'll come by, give you all the supplies you need to fill out a ticket, take the payment, and bring you back any winnings. However, for all this convenience, you may pay a price.

In the first sense, because these people are working to provide you with a service, it's common courtesy to tip them at least a dollar or so every few games, regardless of whether you win or lose. It's probably best to do it the very first time you place an order with them, to encourage good service. And if you win, you should give them a percentage—perhaps 10% on small wins from $10 to $50 and 5% on anything higher. (It's up to you.) Lastly, you should know that the tickets brought in by the runners are the last to be counted before the race closes. Thus, it's possible either that your runner might not make it in time or that the right numbers might not be played. There are no guarantees, so if you're concerned about it, you should probably go to the keno lounge and take care of it yourself.

Unfortunately, no method or system can decrease the house edge in keno. How much you win is directly proportional to your bet size. So there's no advantage to betting more. In fact, if you bet more and win on one of the bigger-spot tickets, it's possible that your theoretical payout could exceed the house limit (usually

Way to Go

The ultimate combination ticket is a "way" ticket. These allow you to circle multiple same-sized groups of numbers in order to create other-sized combinations. For example, you might circle seven different groups of three numbers and want to play all the different possible six-spots. The six-spots would be created by pairing all the three-spot groups. With seven groups to choose from, there'd be twenty-one such possible pairings. Thus your total bet would be $21, "21/6" would indicate the number of combos/spots, and $1 would be your amount per bet.

in the hundreds of thousands of dollars). In that case, you wouldn't be paid properly, actually increasing the house advantage! However, this usually doesn't become an issue until you're betting at least $5 a ticket, picking a dozen numbers, and catching all of them.

In light of not helping your chances, the game does offer some interesting methods of making up a ticket. As opposed to a "straight" ticket where you just choose one group of numbers, "combination" tickets allow you to choose multiple groups using only one piece of paper. For instance, you could mark five numbers, separate two from the other three with a thick line between them, and play any combination of the groupings. That is, the two and the three, the two and the five, the three and the five, or all three possibilities. To play the two-spot and three-spot, you'd put $2 as your total bet, "1/2" and "1/3" as the number of spots marked, and $1 as the price per bet. If all five numbers hit, you'd be paid on both bets, but not the (higher paying) five-spot catch-all. To get paid on that one, you would need to have included "1/5" in there and adjusted your bet.

Naturally, as the number of combinations increases, the more complicated the ticket can get (and the more likely you might be to miss one). For instance, you could add a group of six numbers to the above example. In that case, you'd want to circle the groups of two, three, and six spots. (The spots don't have to be right next to each other, just X'ed and circled.) You'd then have the option of betting on two, three, five, six, eight, nine, and/or eleven spots all at once. If you want to make it really complicated, you can circle certain numbers in more than one group or single numbers (sometimes called "king" numbers) by themselves, which quickly adds multiple possible combinations.

For players who like to feel like they've covered all their bases, there's a special type of play. By drawing a horizontal line that separates the upper and lower numbers and then vertical lines between each column, it's possible to create a 190-way eight-spot ticket! That is, a hundred and ninety ways to pair all the groups of four to form eight-spots. Don't be fooled into thinking you're guaranteed to win anything. In fact, since you need to catch at least four out of every eight to get paid anything, you could theoretically lose all 190 bets if only one number from each of the twenty groups of four were drawn! To tempt you to make this sucker bet, most casinos will allow you to bet less than the usual minimum per bet.

In the end, there's no trick to keno, no magic formula by which you'll tend to hit more often. It's simply a slow game with staggering odds and high house advantages. In fact, the chances of catching twenty out of twenty spots are millions—or possibly billions—of times worse than hitting most slot jackpots. Video keno machines are the only keno version that sometimes approaches reasonable. But with the same horrible odds and only slightly better payouts, at best they're able to yield house advantages that approach those of ordinary slots, which isn't saying much.

Keno: Things to Bear in Mind

• Like slots, this game has a built-in "for" factor—you give your money and only make a profit if you win more units than you bet.

• When indicating a ten-spot as a grouping, rather than writing "1/10," the special notation "1/X" is used.

• It's possible to get paid if none of your spots catch if you pick a lot of numbers and it's likely for at least one of them to be drawn.

> "Each misfortune you encounter will carry in it the seed of tomorrow's good luck."
> —*Og Mandino (1923–1996), U.S. editor and writer*

Every October in Las Vegas, the Global Gaming Expo— "G2E"—showcases all the newest developments in the industry. In recent times, an onslaught of new slots has dominated the expo, but some new table games are introduced each year as well.

The trick in getting a new table game accepted is in preserving a delicate balance. In order for people to play them, they need to be fun and easy and offer a minimal house edge. And in order for the game to find its way onto the floor in the first place, it has to present a way for the casino to make money. The best way to accomplish both is to create a game that's already somewhat familiar, has a relatively low house edge (compared to other games), and can be played quickly (so the casino makes an hourly profit).

Poker 21 was invented by Ferris and Max Zahedi—two brothers from Vancouver, British Columbia—and is just starting to see some play. The game uses a special fifty-three-card deck, which includes a joker that's wild in the poker hand. For the blackjack hand, jacks are worth two, queens three, kings four, and everything else what it normally is. Players can bet on either or both hands, in addition to a bonus side bet (based on how good the poker hand is). The object is to beat the dealer on the blackjack hand and/or qualify with a winning poker hand without getting more than six cards or a total over 21. No splitting, surrendering, or insurance options exist, but the hitting, double-down, and payouts are more liberal. The shift in thinking will be a shock for steady blackjack players, but it is a fun two-in-one game to play.

21+3 is another blackjack-related offshoot. It was created by Derek Webb (the inventor of Three-Card Poker), was first tested at Bally's in Tunica, Mississippi, and is enjoying some success throughout the Midwest. It's basically regular blackjack, but with an optional side bet on the three-card hand formed between the player's first two cards and the dealer's up card. The three-card hand pays off 9 to 1 if it ranks higher than a pair, which will happen just under 9% of the time. So it's not the greatest side bet in the world, but it's certainly not the worst either! If nothing else, the novelty of seeing two very different games played together without interfering with each other is fun.

221 is another Webb invention. Despite the "21" in the name, it actually has nothing to do with blackjack. It's basically a three-in-one, five-card, no-push, no-commission version of pai gow poker. Players break up the five cards they're dealt into a two-card high hand, which has to outrank their two-card middle, which in turn must outrank their single-card low. The bet for each of the three hands is independent. If your high beats the dealer's high, you win that bet regardless of what happens with the others. The middles and lows are figured similarly, with any ties, or "copies," going to the dealer. Copies work similarly as in regular pai gow, they just don't tend to happen as often or have the same direct impact in this game. That impact is what creates the house edge in 221 while allowing players to not have to pay a commission when they win.

357 is another three-in-one game you may come across. As you might guess, it's based on three-, five-, and seven-card poker. After players place bets on each of the three spots, they're each dealt three cards and the dealer sets four cards facedown in front of herself. The three-card hand plays and pays out like the pair plus bet in Three-Card Poker. The dealer turns over two of the four down cards, allowing players to form their five-card hands. Any hands with at least a pair of sixes are paid out according to a schedule. The dealer then turns over the other two table cards. Players need at least two pair with one pair tens or higher to qualify for a win. The building of multiple hands and changing dynamics definitely make 357 an interesting one to try.

Unfortunately, tons of fun-looking games didn't make this section. For instance, a bevy of other blackjack variations, brand games such as Caribbean Draw Poker, as well as four-card versions of poker, variants of craps that use cards, and many more. Just remember the fundamentals you learned about all the casinos' primary games and feel free to give any of these a whirl!

GLOSSARY

Bag English casino term for "thousand," based on the Cockney rhyme of "bag of sand" and "grand."

Blinds In poker, forced bets based on players' positions.

Board In poker, community cards dealt faceup in the center of the table; in keno, the display that shows which numbers came up.

Boat In poker, another term for a full house (three of a kind with a pair).

Brush Cardroom employee responsible for managing the seating list.

Bug In cards, this is a joker able to represent any card; or in pai gow poker, just an ace or to fill a straight or flush.

Bust To lose in general; in blackjack, to have a total more than 21 or "break."

Button In poker, a small plastic disk placed in front of a different player each hand to designate the dealer position.

Cage In sic bo or chuck-a-luck, the wire tumbling device in which the dice are rolled; also the name of the area in the casino where players exchange chips for cash.

Call In poker, to match a bet; in keno and bingo, to draw a number for the game.

Carousel A group of slot machines positioned in a ring, enabling a change clerk to stand in the center.

Casino rate A reduced price on hotel rooms offered to loyal casino customers.

Catch In poker, to get a needed card; in keno, to match a certain number of chosen spots.

Check In poker, to pass the bet; also another name for a gambling chip.

Cheese In poker, really bad cards.

Color up When a player leaving a game exchanges smaller-denomination chips for larger-denomination chips.

Crew In craps, the dealers assigned to the game.

Croupier French for "dealer"; used primarily in baccarat and roulette.

Down to the felt To have no more chips left on the table; broke.

Draw In poker, to receive another card, or a hand that needs a particular card (e.g., a "straight draw"); another name for a tie.

Drop How much the casino makes on a game; in poker, to fold or lose money.

Fill When a slot machine hopper runs out, an attendant gets a bag of coins from the cashier and replenishes it.

Fish An inexperienced and/or poor player, especially in poker as referred to by more experienced players. "If you can't find the fish at the table, you're it!"

Foul In pai gow poker, to set a hand improperly so that the two-card hand is higher than the five-card hand, causing an automatic loss.

Front line In craps, the pass line.

George A good tipper.

Hand In cards, referring to either the particular cards held or all the cards, betting, and action between shuffles.

Hit In general, have a favorable outcome in making a hand or winning a jackpot; in blackjack, to take a card.

Hold In video poker, keeping a card; the overall percentage or dollar amount a casino keeps from a game, table, or machine.

House The meaning of the Italian *casino*.

Juice The money taken as the "rake" in a game (also known as the "vig").

Layout The cloth on a gaming table with markings that give players information such as how to play or where to place their bets.

Load up To play the maximum number of coins per spin that a slot machine or video game will allow.

Marker A check that can be written at the gaming tables by a player who has established credit with the casino.

Mechanic A dealer adept at cheating in cards.

Monkey In blackjack, a card valued at ten; also refers to $500.

Natural The best possible immediate outcome for the player; in blackjack, a two-card hand of 21 points; in baccarat, a two-card total of 8 or 9; in craps, a 7 or 11 on the come-out roll; in video

poker, a royal flush without any wild cards.

Nut Financially, the overhead costs of running a casino or fixed amount a gambler tries to win in a day; the best possible hand in a round of poker (e.g., five same-suited cards ace-high would be a "nut flush").

Paint In poker, a jack, queen, or king; a "picture" or "face" card.

Pay cycle A theoretical expression of the number of plays required for a machine to cycle through all possible winning and nonwinning combinations.

Pit An area of the casino where a group of table games is arranged, at the center of which the dealers and other casino personnel operate.

Pot In poker, the amount of money that accumulates in the middle of the table as each player antes, bets, and raises and which goes to the winner(s) of the hand.

Press When a player lets a winning wager ride with the next bet.

Prop Short for "proposition"; in poker, a player paid by the cardroom to keep shorthanded games going; in craps, a type of bet.

Railbird A kibitzer or spectator who watches a game but doesn't play; if lending support to a particular player, it is known as "sweating" him.

Rake In poker, the flat fee or percentage of the pot the casino

charges each hand in order to make money.

Red, green, and black The most common colors for $5, $25, and $100 chips.

RFB The free room, food, and beverages that high rollers are treated to.

Set In pai gow poker, the way the player divides his seven cards into five-card and two-card hands; in regular poker, another term for "trips" or "three of a kind."

Shill An employee of the gaming establishment acting as a regular player to get the action up.

Shoe A plastic or wooden container that holds multiple decks of cards for dealing.

Spot In keno, a particular number from 1 to 80 that a player selects or the number of numbers that player selects.

Suit One of the four divisions of cards (hearts, spades, diamonds, clubs) in a deck; another term for personnel other than dealers, such as pit bosses and floormen, who work in the pit area.

Surrender In blackjack, Casino War, and certain forms of roulette, to concede the hand by giving up half your wager.

Tilt A malfunctioning slot machine; in poker, a player playing wildly out of frustration.

Toke A gratuity given to a dealer or casino cocktail waitress in cash or chips.

Trips In poker, three of a kind.

Whale How casinos refer to a high roller or big spender.

Wheel The device spun in roulette, slots, and big six to determine an outcome; in poker, a five-high straight that is considered both high and low.

White meat Profit.

World In craps, a bet that the next roll of the dice will total 2, 3, 7, 11, or 12; also called a "whirl."

ACKNOWLEDGMENTS

I am continually grateful for the love and support of my parents Steve and Elaine, sister Marni and grandparents Stanley & Muriel and David & Sara.

I appreciate the help of friends Barry Wood, Bob Ford, Andy Bilbao, Hylah Hill, Heather and Andrew Wenzel.

A special thanks to Becca Michel, Charlie Nikkel, Rafael Alvarez and David at Barona Valley Ranch Resort & Casino for their hospitality. As well as to Danny Jones for sharing his time and knowledge.

To all the friends who've inspired me to make that (planned or last-minute) 3-hour, 52-minute drive across the Mojave. (You know who you are.)

A big thanks to the folks at AMS.

And last but not least, thanks for the patience and hard work of Martin, Frank, Cheryl, Diane, David, Sean and everyone else at PRC who made this project a reality.

Picture Acknowledgments:

All illustrations © Chrysalis Image Library/Mark Franklin

Photography:
© Chrysalis Image Library/Simon Clay 6, 28.
© Gala Casinos 14, 18, 24, 26, 70.
© Las Vegas News Bureau/LVCVA 10, 12, 13, 65.
© MGM Mirage 31.
© PhotoDisc 168.